SHE SELLS EFFORTLESSLY

JANE BAKER

AND CO.

CONTENTS

DEDICATION

This one's for you,
For me,
For all of us.
The ones who were told they'd never make it;
The ones who were told they were too quiet;
Too loud;
Too ambitious;
Too anything.
None of that has to define us.
What other people think or see doesn't have to be our truths.
We might once have been told we were not good enough, or not
loud enough, or any of those labels. That doesn't have to stay
with us and define our futures.
I was written off.
I was trouble.

I was too much of everything and not enough of everything else.

I wasn't understood.

I didn't belong.

And yet I made it.

You're here reading my second published book.

So this one's for us.

For all of us.

For every voice that isn't being heard in the world.

For every person who's hiding because they don't feel enough.

For every person who's been brave enough to blaze their own path.

For every voice that's standing for something.

For every person who's trying, despite having no proof that they can.

Here's to us.

Here's to all of us.

Here's to the amazing world we can build together.

Here's to all of the dreams we bring to life.

Jane Baker

INTRODUCTION

"What if you loved selling?"

"What if making high-ticket sales was as easy as breathing?"

How you currently feel about sales and your beliefs around high-ticket determines your response to both of those questions. For some of you it may be a 'fuck, yes' but for others the idea of loving sales or that sales can be as easy as breathing might seem as if I'm coming from another planet.

It's crazy that I'm writing a book about sales and selling, given the fact that if you'd asked me fifteen years ago I'd have told you, "I can't sell."

I was the shy kid. I was the kid whose school report always included, "Needs to be more outgoing and participate in class discussions." I hated speaking to strangers (unless fuelled by drink as a teenager). I was the total opposite of someone you'd ever imagine loving sales and being pretty bloody epic at selling too. (Yes, I'm tooting my own horn, because that's how I roll!)

And yet here I am. That is exactly who I am, and the reality is I am shit hot at selling. I can sell five, six and even seven figure offers/services with my eyes closed, but not in the traditional way, not in the ways you may have previously thought of when it comes to selling. In fact, I break almost every single mould out there of what a sales expert and salesperson should be.

This is exactly what you're going to see inside this book. If you're looking for sales scripts or any of the traditional sales tactics then this isn't going to be for you. I stand against all of that. I take selling and sales and I strip it down to the very basics; I take sales and selling and turn it into something that every single individual can fall in love with, in their own way. That's why you're here and that's why you need to read this book.

You're done seeing sales how the rest of the world may see it. You're done feeling as if you have to sell in a way that doesn't align with you and you're so over sales feeling hard. That's the journey I'm going to take you on.

We're going to go from wherever you are right now with sales and selling and transform your relationship with it. By the end of this book you'll see sales as the empowering activity it is and the statements above will be your truths.

That's a bold claim, I know. I'm not afraid of making bold claims. It's who I am: I'm the 'go big or go home' type of person and I'm not afraid of saying it.

One of the reasons I'm writing this book in the first place is because I'm so tired of day after day seeing people afraid of selling, not enjoying selling or just not selling at all because they're afraid.

Because they've seen those rants from others online about how they're sick of being "spammed".

Because they've got a sales process that doesn't fit them at all, is totally out of alignment, but they think it's the only way they can make sales.

Because they're trying to make their round peg fit in someone else's square hole sales process.

Because sales is something that is hidden in the shadows, not really shouted about.

Because sales is seen as something you shouldn't embrace, because if you did you'd be just a money grabber.

Yep, all of those things drive me absolutely insane and are why I'm writing this book.

It's all bullshit, and I'm ready to rip it the hell up, show you a new way and change the reputation of "sales" in the process.

So… ready to begin your sales transformation?

Chapter One

LET'S CLEAR A FEW THINGS UP

*T*his book is about sales and selling of high-ticket (even though it's applicable to any level) so before we dive into the juicy sales revolution, let's clear up a few myths around high-ticket. It doesn't matter how you feel about sales if you're going to be held back from high-ticket because of some myths you have around it.

1 High-ticket is more pressure and more work

Here's a real fun fact. I hear from my big high-ticket clients less than I hear from those who work with me at lower levels. Yep... I work less with a 200k client than I do a 6k one! That might sound a little crazy to you right now but it's true and so when I hear people say that high-ticket is more work and more pressure I genuinely laugh, because I don't see it. I don't see it in my own personal experience or with my clients.

So how does this work? People assume that higher pricing means more demand. The classic, "They'll want blood from you if you charge those prices," couldn't be further from the truth, though. The reality is that if someone was going to be demanding and need babysitting, they wouldn't be working with me. I wouldn't accept them as a client because I don't work with those types of people.

I think people forget that you get to decide who you work with. You set your boundaries when it comes to who you say yes to and who you don't. Why would you work with someone who would demand every minute of your time? Why would you say yes to someone who would need babysitting and be incredibly demanding, if that wasn't the type of person you wanted to work with?

You get to decide who you work with.

You set your own rules.

You set the boundaries of working with you.

You get to decide what's acceptable and what isn't.

You get to decide who you want to spend your time with and who you don't.

You are fully in control of all of that and if you've got everything else set up right, you should have filtered the wrong fit people out so they don't even attempt to enter your world.

Let's look at the idea of 'more pressure'. The only reason something would feel like more pressure is because you're choosing that as a belief. Why would there actually be more pressure?

What does more pressure even look like?

Isn't more pressure just you thinking that because the value of what you're selling is higher, you have to put a larger level of pressure on yourself to over deliver, to be amazing, to live up to the expectation that you've set for yourself?

The 'more pressure' isn't actually about those buying from you: it's firmly about you. It's what you have swimming around in that head of yours when you think about someone paying you 5k, 10k, 20k or even six figures.

The pressure you feel is the pressure you put on yourself. Here's a mind-blowing concept... I feel more pressure with lower ticket than I ever do with high-ticket. With low-ticket I don't have control over what they're doing with what they hear and see. I'm not there to guide them and I pride myself on helping people achieve amazing things. With low-ticket I'm out of control. That's my level that I've set for myself, which results in me feeling the pressure with low-ticket more than high.

And it's the same for you. That pressure is just because it's what you're setting for yourself. It's what you're making it all mean. It's not the truth. In reality, the pressure doesn't exist. The only way the pressure exists is because you make it so. You make it your truth.

2 High-ticket is only possible working 1:1. I don't want to be working 24 hours a day, seven days a week

You and me both. This is why I don't, and no, it's definitely not just 1:1.

One of the reasons I love high-ticket is because it's flexible. It can be so many different things to different people. To me it can be one thing but to you it can be something else. It's not one size fits all. It's not an 'it has to look like this' type of thing.

Why can't an online course be high-ticket? The reality is, it can be. I have clients that charge 10k+ for online courses... yes, really!

Why can't a group be high-ticket? It can be: several of my high-ticket offers are exactly that.

Why can't... you get the picture. The reality is that every offer you see can also be leveraged with the high-ticket model.

Whether we're talking 1:1, groups, events, courses, hybrid versions, masterminds, etc., they can all be leveraged as part of the high-ticket model. I've even worked with hairdressers and helped them leverage high-ticket offers.

The idea that something has to be done just one way doesn't work for me. I can't stand the whole cookie cutter approach that says it has to look exactly like this and it has to look like this for everyone. It simply isn't true and it puts so many limitations on people.

Why limit what something can be? Why limit the possibilities of something or someone?

We don't have to, and it's actually something I talked about in my first book (She Lives Limitlessly), which, by the way, if you haven't read and you want to be leveraging the high-ticket model in your business, then I highly recommend checking that out. I take you through how I leveraged high-ticket to unlock my limitless life and how you can too.

But this idea that you have to work just one way, otherwise it can't be high-ticket, is just crazy. Also, the idea that the only way to unlock time freedom in your business is to sell something passive or low-ticket is just not true.

You can unlock the same time freedom, if not more in some people's cases, by taking a different approach. Remember: I said that I spend less time with my high-ticket clients than I do with those working with me on different levels. My clients who are selling high-ticket work on average no more than three to four hours a day, three to four days a week, and if they wanted to work less they absolutely could.

Much like everything else, it comes down to how you choose to set things up, the boundaries you put in place and how you actually make the sales.

This is what this book is about. We're taking sales and we're not just going to have you fall in love with selling but also simplify it. Did you know that just by simplifying your sales you can save yourself hours a month or even a week?

Ready to find how?

"She left her doubts, worries and fears at the door, opened her mind and grew in ways she never knew possible."

Before we dive in properly, I'd love for you to do something. Leave every preconceived belief or idea you have around selling and high-ticket right here on this page.

Yes, you have doubts.

Yes, you have fears.

Yes, you have voices that tell you it's not possible for you.

Yes, you have voices that say you can't.

Yes, you might think you're crap at selling.

But whatever is floating around in your head, whatever voices, fears, beliefs or stories you have playing, let's switch them off for this book.

Let's turn off the voices. Turn down the fears. And instead allow yourself to be open to something new.

Open to changing. Open to seeing something different. Open to being different. Open to growing in a way you may not have considered before.

The only way to change is to let go of what we're holding on to. Right now you may think you'll never change how you feel about selling. You might think that you'll never love it, it'll never be easy or that you're just no good at selling.

But there's only one way we're going to change any of that and it's for you to be open to it changing.

So turn it all off. Tell it you're busy. Let's open that mind to new possibilities and grow.

Chapter Two

MY STORY

I realise that some of you may be here after reading my first book and so you'll be familiar with much of this. Those who are brand new to me, though, may be wondering, what's the backstory of Jane?

Have you ever had this moment when you're in a room full of people and yet you feel as if you're all alone? That was me. I always knew I was destined for more, that I was here to do more, but it took me a few years to figure out what that looked like and to do something about it.

Life wasn't straightforward for me growing up. I always had that feeling of not belonging, of being destined for more. I couldn't explain what 'more' looked like but I knew I was different.

I left school at sixteen without a single qualification to

my name, not one. Most would have resigned them-selves to a life with not much hope. I didn't, but the world around me did. Everyone and their dog seemed to want to tell me what I should do with my life. Opinions and voices were thrown at me from all angles, but they all pretty much said the same thing. Go get a job and settle into life.

It sounded like hell. But off I went at sixteen to my first job in a call centre. I lasted six weeks. Not because I couldn't do it, but because apparently, standing up to a manager who was clearly wrong wasn't appropriate and so I was let go. After this short experience of dipping my toe into the working world, I moved to London with my step sister and my now husband. I was seventeen at the time and when I think about that now it's totally crazy. It was here that I had my eyes opened. I'd walk down Oxford Street and around the Ritz imagining myself living that life, in the designer shops picking up every-thing, sipping champagne and celebrating an amazing day.

It opened my eyes to a world I knew existed but had never been involved with. I got to see the world through a new pair of eyes and it further ignited the feeling inside myself that I was born for more. I knew I belonged in those circles. I knew I belonged in that space even though at that moment in time I couldn't have been further out of them. I had no job, no money and no direction at all. I just knew I'd be going somewhere.

At eighteen I moved back to Wales but I fell pregnant. Cue the disappointed comments and eye rolls; here's the eighteen year old who didn't go back to education, has no qualifications, no job and now she's pregnant. Even if they didn't always say it out loud, I knew it's what they were thinking.

At our twenty week scan we were given the news that all was not ok. What would follow would be weeks and months of specialist appointments and planning for the series of operations our daughter would have to go through when born. She was diagnosed with Hypoplastic Left Heart Syndrome. I don't think I slept from the moment we were told. I'd spend hours just researching and reading through everything they'd given us. What I didn't know at this moment was that a few months down the line my whole world would change, and that the event that would trigger me into getting myself to where I am now would take place.

At 32 weeks I felt that something wasn't quite right. My husband was working shifts and so I got in touch with my mother. She suggested we go to the hospital just as a precaution.

On arrival I got hooked up to all those machines and I feared the worst, but then over the monitor came the sound of the heartbeat that I'd heard so many times. I was relieved, but I was quickly informed that they weren't happy and had arranged a conference call with all of the consultants and professors that had so far been involved with my case. But still, she was ok, and so I was taken off the monitors and told to relax while they all made their decisions. I lay there with no idea what was to come next.

They wanted to do a scan and to take some measurements before they made their final decision on how to progress. I wasn't worried. I'd not long heard the heartbeat so what was there to worry about, right? But ten minutes later I was given the news that no one ever wants to hear. The words that would stay etched in my memory forever were said to us: "I'm sorry, but there's no heartbeat."

And that was that. The 32 weeks during which I'd lain there with all of those dreams and hopes for her life… gone. No one really knows how it feels until it's them. You see it on TV programmes and read about it in magazines, but it never crossed my mind that it would be my reality. That was me, the one whose baby had died.

A few days later I was taken into hospital to deliver her.

Walking out of the hospital later that day with nothing other than an A5 booklet with prints, pictures and hair was nothing short of heartbreaking.

It was a completely horrific, tragic moment in my life, but it would lead me to where I am today. It was my life defining moment.

I wanted more from life. I wanted my life to really mean something. I didn't want to spend my life feeling as if I didn't belong and that I was destined for more but not doing anything about it. I didn't want to settle, I wanted to live a complete limitless life and I wanted the family that I knew I would have one day to live it too. I wanted my daughter's death to stand for something.

I started my first business, without a clue what I was doing, with no experience and no help. I just woke up one morning and said, 'I'm doing this!'

At the time I was planning my wedding. As we didn't have the budget to have everything done for us or have all the fancy companies, we were doing a lot of it ourselves. I sat there one morning thinking, 'What if, instead of just using this stuff for our own wedding, we hired it out to others too?' That's what I did overnight: I started a wedding and event hire business. I had no money to invest and no experience, but I was about to learn that the business world was and is a complete roller coaster.

Within six months we had a full order book and went from just a handful of hire items to a whole catalogue. We were so busy, we were having to turn bookings away. We even had people from all parts of the country who wanted us to provide our services, everywhere from Norfolk to Newcastle and Scotland. By this point I also had two kids under eleven months at home, but I didn't let that stop me. My kids were never ever going to be a distraction and they were never going to be an excuse; they were going to be the reason I did it all and not the reason I didn't!

As amazing as things were at that point, I knew we could do more. My husband came to work in the business as well and I decided it was time to go bigger. Plenty of hotels provided recommendations of companies customers could use and we were listed on most, but I had this idea of being the supplier who wasn't just recommended but that was included in every event the hotels did: corporate, weddings, everything.

I started pitching. I lost count of the number of emails I'd send on a daily basis, but I'd hit all the contact forms and when I ran out of those I'd find other emails. I didn't have any experience in pitching and yet here I was killing it because the responses blew me away. I was about to land a six figure contract with a huge hotel chain after just over one year in business. I learnt that just going for it and doing very little worrying, thinking and debating was the key. I even pitched to the Queen!

Over the next 12-24 months I grew the company even more. We had contracts with hotels worldwide, and we had franchisees across the UK. We were booked solid and things were amazing.

I'm often asked what my secret was. The answer is that I just did it. Most people think of an idea or think of something they'd like to do and then spend ten minutes talking themselves out of doing it. I just did it. I went and got it done. It's one of my biggest pieces of advice for business owners: just go and get it done. Don't give yourself time to get wrapped up in your head and end up talking yourself out of doing something.

Fast forward to 2013. I hated my life. There, I said it! I did hate it: I was working every single day. I never had a weekend off or even a day off. I couldn't take holidays. I'd lost all sight of the life I was originally building this for. I had success, sure, but the rest was a mess and I was a mess. I'd totally fallen out of love with what I did, and actually I came to the realisation that I never loved it anyway. It was just something that was there at the time. It was never a passion and I certainly never enjoyed it. I decided drastic action had to be taken.

I left it behind. I walked away without a clue as to what was coming next. I knew I was good at business; I knew I was good at making money; people told me I had that natural talent for business. I could see and think of things that others just couldn't, but honestly, I had no clue what to do for myself at that time.

I was a mentor and coach for various organisations and I genuinely loved it. It turned out I wasn't only good at making things happen for myself, I was particularly good at helping others make lots of money, and so it was suggested to me that I turned my passion into a business. At first I thought they were crazy. I mean, who on earth was going to follow and buy from me? But the more I thought of it, the more it ticked all the boxes that I'd ever set out for myself. It lit a fire inside of me that I'd never felt before and so I took the plunge.

In October 2013 I launched my coaching business The Women's Business Academy. They say 'the rest is history', only it wasn't! Cue six months of no sales. I drove myself insane. I mean, I knew business. I knew how to make sales. I was shit hot at making sales and yet I was sucking and for ages I couldn't figure out why. I was following all the experts, I had a coach, I was doing the funnels and freebies and webinars and online courses and low-end offerings. It should have been working but it wasn't.

Six months later I decided enough was enough, I threw out the rule book that others had given me, I threw out all the must dos and must haves that the gurus said, and I went back to basics. I went to what I knew and within a week I'd gone from zero sales to over 15k. I had super-charged my business in just one week. What did I change? I went from online courses and low-end to putting together a high-end package and selling it. I sold out of every space within two weeks.

I quickly grew on that and my sales just kept rising. Six months later I had done over 100k in sales and I helped clients do the exact same thing. No words can describe just how amazing it felt and still does feel to have done it, to have turned it around and more importantly be in a position where I could and still can help others do the same.

It sounds clichéd, but my coaching business gave me my life and happiness back. High-end selling enabled me to truly unlock the freedom that I had spent so long desiring. In fact, I felt freedom on a level I hadn't ever thought would be possible for me, and it lit me up in a way my first business never did. Despite its success it wasn't really for me.

Since launching my coaching business back in 2013 I've entered a whole new period of my life. It's opened doors

I never imagined little old me would be walking through. I can remember being shortlisted for my first Great British Entrepreneur Award as Young Entrepreneur Of The Year and thinking, who me? I'd be lying if I said I never had that voice inside my head saying, "Who the hell are you to be in this position?" but I don't listen to it and have long learnt to just ignore it. I'm here because I deserve to be. I've earned my place and I'm going to enjoy it.

When I started my coaching business I genuinely never intended to go back to other types of business, but in the past few years I've found myself being called in a few different directions. When I really dialled into my dream that word "empire" kept popping up. When I dug into it a bit more I realised that I don't just want to be a coach, I want to own an empire. You might read that thinking *really?* but it's true. I'm not your average coach; I'm not your average person. I have big goals, big dreams and I intend making every one of them my reality.

After discovering and tuning into my bigger dreams, I decided it was time to launch some new businesses, but this time I wouldn't be hands on. As I write this I own three businesses including my coaching business and I genuinely wouldn't have it any other way. I also have a fourth business launching in the next few months. If you have big dreams, no matter how ridiculous they may seem, always go after them.

In 2019 I had the honour of being listed as a top 100 UK female entrepreneur – one of my proudest moments to date.

I love my home town but I didn't belong there. I felt like my wings were clipped and I felt suffocated by a place I didn't belong in. 2019 was the year I decided that enough was enough. Enough talking about it, enough talking about a better life for my three kids: I decided it was time to do it. In August 2019 we made the move from Wales in the United Kingdom and decided to start living island life in Lanzarote, in the Canary Islands. It has been an emotional but extremely rewarding process, and also a huge goal that I just know my younger self is so amazingly proud of us having achieved.

I always say to people that if I can do it then so can you, and it's genuinely how I feel. If you'd told twelve year old me that I'd be living here, doing what I do with the life I have, she'd likely have laughed. Sixteen year old me would have been rolling on the floor laughing.

I'm living proof you can achieve anything despite where you begin in life.

I did. So can you.

MY STORY WITH SELLING

I've decided to write this separately from my main story and journey so that I could take a little time to explain why I'm passionate about selling and to offer an insight into the journey that I've been on with selling. You're about to embark on a book all about selling effortlessly so knowing a little about my experience with selling will probably help!

I'm not about to tell you a story of how I first knew I was an excellent seller when I was six selling crisps on the school yard.

I never did that. I probably could have but I didn't and I'm not one of those people. I can't say I always had this entrepreneurial spirit. I never even considered it as an option for me until that one random day over a decade ago when I started my business on a whim. Until then I'd have said I wasn't a natural entrepreneur; I wasn't a natural salesperson or anything similar. In fact, the only real brush I had with selling was something I hated.

It was during my short time working in a call centre at sixteen. Selling was part of my job and I hated it. I'd stare at the script, thinking... this can't be the best way to do this, surely!

I never sold a single thing, not a thing. I'd probably have said I was a terrible salesperson; in fact, I know I would have.

Yet when I started my business, selling didn't even cross my mind. It sounds crazy as I write this, but it didn't. I just made sales. It happened. I made big sales too. I was selling six figure contracts and packages within a few months of launching.

It wasn't until I started my online coaching business that I really thought about the selling aspect and selling skill. Until that point I had just been doing my thing and doing it extremely well, I might add!

Yet suddenly when I launched that online coaching business I struggled with the whole selling thing. It made no real sense to me as I had made big sales with my eyes closed before. Of course, I thought as it was a different industry that was likely the issue: I just wasn't used to it yet or I didn't know enough; maybe it was because I was too shy. I used to be incredibly shy and wouldn't speak to people as a child. I'm not naturally outgoing so maybe it was because of that.

I signed up for courses and tried selling like everyone else. I tried doing what seemed to work amazingly well for others, only the more I sank down into that hole, the harder sales became. I went from being able to sell six figure offerings with ease to struggling to sell something that was $97. I kid you not!

One day I realised that the issue was that I was going down the hole of thinking that because I didn't sell like everyone else around me, I didn't know how to sell. I could sell, I just didn't do it like everyone else around me or online at the time seemed to be doing – but their way didn't work for me and I hated it.

For the first time since sitting in that call centre, I would dread getting on a sales call with someone. That wasn't something I ever experienced in my first business. During that time, I never compared myself. I never tried to sell someone else's way. I never really saw selling as a skill… I just did it. I did it my way!

In that AHA moment back in 2013, I decided not only was I going to blaze my own path in delivering high-ticket to unlock the freedom I desired but that I'd also blaze my own path in how I made sales.

Whilst others preached webinars and sales pages, I stopped doing them and didn't have any. I took my website down. I even stopped sales calls, and something amazing happened.

When I stepped into my power, when I aligned with my own sales power, when I blazed and embraced my own way, I went from struggling to make any sales to selling 40k with ease, selling 100k cash with ease and from there I've continued forward like a rocket ship.

These days I sell five, six and even seven figures with total ease. I can make a 200k cash sale with ease just like I can make 10k, 50k or even more with ease. What's the secret?

You're going to find out.

Chapter Three

SALES WILL TRANSFORM YOUR LIFE

*S*ales can open so many doors in your life. It can pave the way for you to unlock the life you desire, and yet so many business owners are not just afraid of it but actually avoid it.

In fact, they'll actually avoid selling, they'll avoid ever even mentioning that they have something to sell, and yet they'll often sit there wondering why they're not making sales. It's often because we get drawn into those social media posts – you know, the ones that rant and rave about those messages in their inbox or they're tearing someone else down for trying. I'll be honest, I've done that.

Just like I've got annoyed with the cold caller or seller at the door, often for many of us our brushes with sales don't exactly leave us jumping for joy. Whether it's that cold caller who wouldn't take no for an answer, the sales representative in the shop that followed you everywhere or that random person who jumped into your inbox, your brushes with sales may not have been ones that make you go 'OMG sales is amazing.'

Then when it's backed up with seeing other people's posts tearing sales down or stressing how they're doing a training where they "don't sell" at the end of it, it all comes together to create a picture in your mind that says selling is bad, selling is wrong, selling is something you should avoid doing at all costs.

I call bullshit and I wholeheartedly disagree. In fact, I always have.

I've never once felt like sales was the bad guy. That doesn't mean I haven't lacked confidence or felt fearful of selling, because I have, but I never had this idea that I shouldn't sell, I just saw badly implemented sales strategies or ones that didn't align with the person carrying them out.

Think about that person who's cold calling you – is sales the issue? No, they're trying to stick to a badly put together script with what's quite frankly an outdated strategy. Worse still they're just randomly punching numbers, hoping and praying you'll be someone who's the right fit.

That's not the fault of selling.

That person who's following you around the store, waiting for the perfect opportunity to pounce – is sales the real issue? No, they've been trained and told to do that. In fact, in many cases they think it's good customer service and instead of thinking about people being individuals who buy in different ways, they're told to take the same approach with everyone. In reality, it's a crap strategy and approach.

But is sales at fault? No.

That message that's jumped into your inbox – they've never met you, never spoken with you, and they're trying to sell you something you'd never in a million years be interested in. We all have them, but are they doing something terrible? No, and realistically they don't even know what they're doing. Often they've been provided with a strategy that doesn't work for them or they're just trying to get their business off the ground. Annoying? Yes, but at least they're trying.

Is sales the thing at fault? No.

For every bad experience we may feel that we've had with sales, we will also have had plenty of good experiences, often experiences when we didn't even realise we had been sold to. They don't stay front and centre of our minds because the negative will always take over and often stands out more. Many of the positive experiences we've had will also have been so just natural we won't even associate it with selling.

This is half the issue when you think about it. Selling and sales has been turned into this massive monster and often pictured as something that's really complicated. Many people feel as if they're not really selling if they're not using a script or doing a multitude of other things.

"I don't want people to know I'm trying to make sales"

A new client said that to me once, and I won't lie, my head went a little 'WHAT?!'

Why wouldn't you want people to know you're trying to make sales?

Why wouldn't you want the world to know they can buy from you?

Why wouldn't you want people to know that you have something amazing for them?

Her answers all revolved around fears of what others would think: fear of what people would think if she tried to sell or if anyone knew she was trying to make sales. As if sales was this big bad thing that no business owner should want to do.

It puzzled me. I understand the fear aspect but as a business owner it does perplex me when people don't actually want to sell, and then I remember it's generally because of what they think and see selling as.

If you see something as a monster for long enough, you'll think it is one. If you tell yourself to be afraid of the dark for long enough, you will be.

So it's natural that when you're surrounded by talk of sales being the bad guy, being icky, being wrong, and you associate that with the sales experiences you remember when you feel you were being sold to, it's really quick and very easy to get yourself into a space where sales feels like the worst thing you could ever do.

But what happens when you don't sell? Does anyone benefit?

Let's be real, the only thing that benefits when you don't sell is your own fear. Your fear keeps you in a space where it believes you're safe for sure, but other than that, does anyone else benefit?

Do you benefit?

Does your ideal client benefit?

Does your audience benefit?

Does the world benefit?

No, they don't, because underneath your dreams, underneath your ideal client's needs and wants, lies the need for sales to happen! Sales unlocks the doors to the vast majority of things you're sat there dreaming about, not just for you but for your audience, ideal clients and the lasting legacy you may want to leave.

Think about it this way… every time you *don't* tell someone there's another step for them to take, what happens for them?

Every time you *don't* tell someone that there's something available for them to buy, what happens to your dreams?

Every time you listen to that voice of fear and don't tell the world you have something available, what happens for you, for them and for the world?

Nothing! A big fat ball of nothing happens. Harsh? Yes, but true.

When you don't let someone know that there's something for them, you're holding them back from something they need or want. When you don't sell, you don't take a step forward towards your own dreams. When you don't let the world see what you have, the world misses out on what it needs.

Who are you to deny the world, your audience or your dreams the chance to say yes? Because that's what you're doing, you know.

When you choose to see the negative of sales...When you choose to sit with all those negative stories... When you choose to listen to the fear that tells you not to sell... When you choose to not understand the power of sales and harness it in a way that is perfect for you...

You take away the chance and choice of others to say yes to something they need... You take away the chance for you to make your dreams happen... You take away the chance for someone out there in the big wide world to receive something they need.

Doesn't feel so good when you think of it that way, right? And for what?

Because you put sales in the naughty corner, because you took your experiences or how you see others sell and decided that sales was the thing at fault instead of the way sales was being used.

In the end the only way you'll ever fully serve your audience, the world and your dreams is to SELL.

"Selling is being of service"

It's easy to list all of the things we don't like about selling. It's really easy, because many of us spend a lot of our time talking to others about how much we dislike it.

False scarcity

Scripts

Following me around

Random messages from people I don't know

Being pushy

The list could go on, but for each of those we need to remember that actually it's not sales at fault; it's the way sales is being used and the person implementing that particular sales activity that you don't enjoy and not the sales itself.

If we think about sales, just as the pure sales aspect, we'd see that it's really none of the above. Sales is giving someone the opportunity to buy something from you that they need or want.

It's not the spam messages.

It's not the cold calls.

It's not the pushy feeling.

It's just an invitation to walk through a door, whatever that door may be for you. By giving someone the opportunity to walk through the door so much can change, not just for you but for them too. Think about it, when someone is given that invitation to walk through and they say yes, what changes for them?

So for my clients it can change:

Their relationships and family experiences

The amount of time they have to enjoy living their life

The amount of money they make

The dream items they can buy

The dream holidays they can go on

The dream homes they can buy

The job they can quit

The wider family they can hire

Their stress levels

Their happiness

The level of confidence and belief they have in themselves

What can change for me:

I've been able to help someone and truly be of service

I've been able to take my own family to experience things I once dreamt of

I've been able to unlock time freedom

I've become happier

I've been able to move my family to live a dream life that once would never have been possible

I can fly on private jets

I can eat at the most amazing places

I can further invest in my own growth

What can change for the world:

It can witness someone else changing their life

It can witness someone else living out their true purpose

It can witness someone else unlock their limitless life

Which has the most impact? The not selling or the selling?

Yes, there's only one clear winner. It's *not* shutting up and stopping the world seeing that you have something. It's *not* shutting up and stopping someone in your audience receiving the thing they really need and want.

Selling is where you're going to make the most impact!

"Free isn't enough for most"

You may be thinking at this point that if you give enough free stuff then people will value it enough and then they'll reach out to you and want to work with you, which means you'll never actually have to mention that you sell anything.

I mean, you could, but isn't that selling anyway?

It's just putting the responsibility of initiating the selling element on them. It would still be you actually closing the sale, it would still be you actually doing the selling, but instead of you being the one in control of those sales being able to happen, you're leaving the responsibility for the sale to happen on them. This will then also mean you don't have control over your sales.

It's worth noting that while a percentage of people will reach out to you, there's a larger percentage of them who won't, and in fact they'll go somewhere else and buy from someone who has told them, "Hey, you can actually buy from me."

Whilst they do end up getting the full service they need, you end up missing out.

The other question about 'free' is, do people ever really get what they need?

You may be surprised to find out that for a large number of people free just doesn't hit the spot. I'm one of those people and so are most of those who work with me. Free doesn't mean people are going to value it. Whilst a small section of them will, of course, there's a larger section who won't, and the small section who do value the free will still need more in order to receive what they really need.

Think about it... free is only ever going to take someone so far. I know that I don't fully get what I need until I'm actually paying for it, because it's the paying for it that means I commit to it. It's the paying for it that means I'm going to put myself in a place where the transformation, support or service I need can fully be delivered and I can fully flourish and get what I need.

Providing your audience with free stuff is, of course, being of service to some degree, but how much of a service? Also, for some of you it may actually be doing more harm than good. In later chapters we'll cover how free might just be putting off the very people you want to be selling to and how free might be complicating a whole sales process and making sales feel really hard.

But if we stay with the aspect of whether free is beneficial to your business or not, there's still the very real reality that when you just wait for others to come and ask to buy from you, never letting anyone in the whole wide world know that they can buy from you, you are directly putting the opportunity to make sales in someone else's hands.

You're not in control. You're not in the driving seat. You're sitting there, waiting, hoping that someone will reach out and say, "Hey, how can I work with you?"

But people aren't mind readers and many people will jump to the conclusion that you simply have nothing for sale because you've never mentioned it. They'll love your free content because you're putting it out there, but they'll never think about buying from you because you've simply never told them or given them the idea that they can.

I can to this day still remember the exact moment a client had a massive AHA moment just from this. The turning point for her going from no sales to over 100k in under twelve months was the moment she realised she had never let her audience know they could buy from her.

We were on our first call and she was telling me how everyone seemed to love her content but no one had ever bought. She had finally decided to have a conversation with one of her long term and most engaged followers to see if she needed anything that she could help with, and she was so shocked to hear the reply, "I love your content. I actually started working with xyz a few months ago and it's been amazing."

When she was sharing this with me she was coming from a place of being a little annoyed. She said, "I spend all this time sharing free information and this is what they do. They love my content but never buy anything from me…" I could feel her frustration, but I simply asked, "When was the last time you mentioned being able to work with you, even in passing?"

Her answer was *never*.

And it was in that moment that she realised she had never even opened a space for the sales to happen. She had never given them the opportunity to know there was a next step to take with her.

With one simple small change, she started to make sales so easy she couldn't believe she'd been putting off doing it before.

We shouldn't assume that everyone knows they can work with you just because you show up with free content. We shouldn't assume that just because they enjoy that free content they're going to fall over themselves wanting to work with you and we shouldn't assume that everyone who wants to work with you is going to reach out and ask you.

Why would you want to leave any of that chance? Why would you want to leave to chance the opportunity for someone to grow, to transform, to receive exactly what they need or want? Why wouldn't you want to let them know that you're there, to be of full service?

Ultimately that's what selling always is. It's you opening a door and saying, would you like to walk through and receive the full service of what you need and want?

Selling is not that big bad wolf. It is not the crappy messages. It's not cold calling. It's not any of those things sales has been labelled. Sales is you having a conversation, opening up an invitation and doing it in a way that's right for you which enables you to be of full service to your audience, to yourself and to the world, which then enables transformations for everyone at every level.

Don't you deserve that? Doesn't your audience? Doesn't the world?

The short answer is of course yes, you do, they do and the world does.

The world wants you to have more!

That might sound a little extreme but it's true and it's something I want you to think of when it comes to high-ticket selling or effortlessly selling to the point where sales just flow to you.

For some people there's this idea that it's wrong to want more, it's wrong to charge more, and it's a bad thing. Some might even feel like money is a bad thing, but what if that isn't actually the case?

Let's look at the evidence. If you make more money, if you have more money, what would you be doing with it?

If you were to list all of the things you'd do if you had more money, I can almost guarantee that on that list would be things like charity work, helping family, helping others or a multitude of other things, but all of them focusing around the concept of helping others: your money benefitting other people!

That's the thing... when you have more, you can actually do more.

So when people don't sell because they're afraid of having more, that having more might change them, that it's not safe to have more or that it's wrong to even want more, they're actually buying into the belief around money that isn't even real. There's more proof that when you have more, you do more good. Having more would enable you to make a bigger impact. You could make a bigger change not just in your own life but in your wider family's lives or the world, even.

Money isn't a bad thing, yet it's one of the reasons why people don't make sales and sometimes they subconsciously make sales difficult and hold themselves back from charging what they really desire or from offering what they really desire, because they're buying into the belief that having more money will mean they'll change or be bad or that they shouldn't want more.

I say bullshit... having more means you can do more. Having more means the world will benefit. The world wants you to have more, because the more you have, the more change you'll help bring, whether that's small change for those surrounding you or bigger world changes.

By you having more, you can impact more! Isn't that bloody amazing?

And sales have a direct role in you making that happen.

See, the world wants you to be selling and making it rain money. It wants you to make sales so easy that you go and make more every single day. It wants that for you because it knows the difference you will then make in the world, in your own life and in other people's lives!

When you doubt whether you should have more, whether you should charge more, whether it's safe to have more, just remember the world wants you to have it.

Action points:

Make a list of all the negative things you think about sales – all of the things fear says when you think of selling. Then unpack them, write out why it's not actually the "sales" at all. It's the strategy behind it that's not aligned, it's the person who doesn't really know what they're doing, it's the lack of research.

Then think about your ideal clients, yourself and your life, and the world. Just like I did above, write down the changes that are possible for each as a result of selling. What positive changes will happen as a result of people being able to have the opportunity to say yes?

Read it all back and ask yourself, what is sales really? Decide what beautiful thing you want it to be.

Sales is the doorway for an amazing life not just for my clients but for myself and the opportunity for me to leave a lasting legacy in the world.

Chapter Four

EFFORTLESSLY SELLING BEGINS WITH YOU

*P*eople spend years and years searching for a magic bullet, that one question or one phrase that you can use to magically make selling easy, or that one strategy that has everyone banging down your doors and begging to be able to buy from you... but what if the very thing so many people spend years searching for doesn't exist?

That's the truth - it doesn't.

You could take all the sales courses and have all the scripts in the entire world and still feel that making sales is hard, still feel as if every sale you make is like pulling teeth. In reality, effortlessly selling isn't about any of that.

You won't find it in the strategies either. You can have two people implementing the same strategy and one will say how easy it is to make sales and the other will say how it feels so hard and frustrating.

But why?

To unlock selling that feels easy you first have to understand that it is only possible if you are in a space where you believe it's possible.

Step One in achieving this is getting yourself into a space where you actually expect to make sales with complete ease. Now that might sound a little airy fairy to some of you, and I get that, but there's real logic behind it.

Take the sales aspect out of the equation and think about times in your life when you've believed something to be hard before you've even begun it. Has it turned out to be hard? Now think about the things you expect to find really easy in your life. Do they turn out to be easy?

99% of the time you'll find the above to be the case, so why do so many of us believe sales has to be difficult in the first place? It's often down to what we've heard, seen, experienced or picked up on through our years. We're told that selling is a skill, building a successful business is hard work, more businesses fail than succeed, success only comes to those who work hard.

We may even witness other people doing things and they'll share how difficult it is for them. In fact, at any time as you scroll through your social media you'll likely come across plenty of posts that talk about how making sales is hard for them, how growing their business has been hard for them and those are all things we pick up on.

I'm not here to say that building a successful business is a walk in the park where nothing ever goes wrong and happens with your eyes closed overnight without you doing anything because that's genuinely not the case, but it doesn't have to be this long hard slog that we believe either, and when it comes to selling it doesn't have to feel "hard". It doesn't have to feel like pulling teeth every time to get the yes.

It gets to be as easy as we decide it's going to be. It gets to be as easy as we expect it to be.

It's really not down to a magic strategy, to a magic word or phrase; it begins with you and the beliefs you hold, and the expectations you hold around how easy or hard selling has to be for you.

A client of mine once came to me and said that every time she makes a sale she doesn't even feel excited by the sale because it felt so hard and so tiring to get the sale in the first place. She asked what she could say on a call to change that.

We could have created a whole script for her, could have given her a million new phrases to use or questions to ask, but would it really have changed the outcome of the sale feeling hard?

No, because the wheels were set in motion for that sale to be hard long before she got on the sales calls.

In every piece of content she created, she was coming from the place of talking to the people whom she believed she'd be convincing and would spend weeks and hours converting. In every action she took she was acting from the space and the expectation that whatever sales she was going to make was going to be really hard. In every sales call she prepared to go on she was already in the space of expecting that sale to feel hard or to not convert them at all. That's what happens with our expectations and thoughts - they trickle over into our actions, into the energy that we take into things and the results that we see.

So we didn't come up with a sales script; we didn't look at new phrases or questions she could ask; we simply started by changing the very first thing that needed changing and that was the expectation and belief that every sale had to be hard.

It's not easy when you don't necessarily have proof that it's the case. If the only sales you have made have been hard, you're likely thinking, "but I have no proof it can be easy." In reality though, you had no proof that sales had to be hard.

The only proof the vast majority of us ever had about sales being hard is what we heard from others, saw with others, experienced through others. We took on their beliefs, their experiences and their thoughts without any actual proof and made them our own.

It's actually quite funny when you think about it. We'll take something negative on board or something not quite so good without any real proof, but when it comes to something more positive we're often far more likely to sit back and say, "I have no proof that it's true so I can't believe it."

And of course, because you've been acting from that negative space, you are also far more likely to have then had proof yourself that backs up that belief. The more you act from the space that says sales must be hard, the more you'll see that to be true and so then you believe you have all the proof in the world to show that sales for you must be hard.

You still want sales to feel easier though. You still want it to be easy and you see others sharing how easy sales is for them and you think that they must have the magic bean for you, the magic strategy to change how hard making sales is for you.

But it doesn't work. It doesn't ever change anything for you. Different strategies, same hard feeling. Because ultimately, the sales feeling isn't something your strategy has necessarily created but rather you're seeing it because you believed it had to be that way to begin with.

Of course, you don't necessarily have proof that sales can be easy for you. We know that you've probably gathered more proof to say that sales must be hard and so now you're thinking, how do I know that sales can actually be easy for me?

You have two options.

1. You took on the notion of sales needing to be hard for you based on what others have told you, what you may have heard over the years, and experiences other people have experienced. You then perhaps acted from the space of sales needing to be hard and so you ended up seeing that sales were indeed hard. This then gave you further proof in your mind and cemented that idea in. But you know, for every "making sales is so hard" or "success is so hard" person, there is someone out there sharing a different experience.

They're sharing their experiences where sales flow to them with total ease, where they don't ever feel as if making the sale is difficult or like pulling teeth. Sales is effortless for them and they're out there sharing the experiences of that. I'm one of those people!

What if you took our experiences on as your proof instead? If you once took on someone's negative experience or beliefs with sales as your proof that sales has to be hard, why can't you take on our experiences and beliefs as your proof that sales can be SO easy?

Remember you didn't have any proof in the beginning to back up your belief that sales had to be hard: the only proof you received was *after* you acted from that belief space.

So what if you took the fact that people like myself, my clients and many others out there are living proof that sales can also be so freaking easy, that selling can be effortless and see it as proof that you CAN too!

The fact that we can is proof that you can; you just haven't decided to make it your belief yet. You haven't decided to step in and have the expectation that selling is effortless and that making sales is so easy for you, and because you haven't stepped into that belief yet, you're not seeing the proof on the other side for you. Simply, you're not acting from the space where you'd even expect to make sales easy. If you're not acting from that space, you won't be taking the action, acting with the energy or anything else that is the first step to make it possible for you to make sales with ease.

2. Maybe you're thinking that just knowing that others can isn't enough for you to believe that it's actually possible for you too. I get that, especially if you're someone who hasn't had any experiences that would ever lead you to believe that selling can be easy, that making sales can be easy and that people love to buy from you.

It can be difficult to take that belief on. You have so much proof that it's just not the case and it can be hard to believe that it could ever be possible for you without completely changing something. Nothing will change if you just change the belief you have around this - at least that might be what you're thinking to yourself.

"Sure Jane, easy for you to say that sales can be easy. It's easy for you to say *just believe*."

I'm going to level with you. I'm not for one second saying that all you ever have to do is change what you believe and you'll magically get the results. I'm not saying that all you need to do is read this one chapter, change your beliefs and *voila* you'll make sales with ease.

For some of you that might actually be the case, but for many of you there will of course be other changes you may have to make; small ones for some, bigger ones for others. It may be that a small change in your strategy is needed, it may be you're selling the wrong thing, it may be you need every chapter in this book but the key thing here is that NONE of what you read or take action on from any other chapter will make an ounce of difference to how you feel about selling, how you feel about how you make sales or how you feel about how hard or easy it is unless you change the belief you hold around that in the first place.

It's not about saying you could magically decide to just believe sales is easy and *boom* you'd have tons tomorrow without lifting a finger, but it is about saying and understanding that something will never ever be easy or flow unless you're in a space where you believe that it's not just possible for you but that you expect it to be that way too.

So what if you just decided it was going to be easy? What if right now you decided, "You know what? Sales is going to be easy. Selling is going to be easy. I expect to attract people who can't wait to buy from me."

Because you can, you know. You could decide all of that right now. You could decide that it is going to be your truth from now on, it is going to be 100% what you believe and receive. You don't need a ton of proof. You don't need proof from me. From the world. Even from yourself.

You can decide to change what you expect at any given moment. You can decide to change what you believe about how easy something has to be for you without an ounce of proof.

I did. In fact, I wouldn't be here if I had waited for proof to show me that I could.

I didn't know anyone who had ever started a business, let alone built a successful one. I wasn't surrounded by people who believed in themselves. I come from an area which is largely classed as deprived (I hate that word).

But remember in my story I told you that I had always known two things. I was going to be Rich and a Celebrity (not in the clichéd type of way). I had no idea how. I had no idea doing what. I had no proof whatsoever. But I knew, regardless of any of that, I would be. I didn't need proof. I didn't need anyone else to tell me or show me that I could. I decided for myself that I could.

I decided to believe in myself. I decided to step into a space with complete, unshakeable belief about myself, and because I did that I ended up taking action from that space that I otherwise would not have taken.

Because I took that action, because I embodied the energy of I CAN, I got to where I am today. I received because I first believed and expected I would.

So you don't need proof to change your belief, to expect something different. You can just choose to decide. Just like you decided that sales had to be hard, you can choose the opposite. Just like you decided that selling had to be difficult, you can choose the opposite. You get to decide, so decide based upon what you want to see, feel and experience.

"It's the same at any level" (high-ticket selling is just as easy)

But selling high-ticket must be more difficult, mustn't it?

You don't sell 10k, 20k, 50k or even 100k+ with ease! Right?

Wrong!

Just because the price changes doesn't mean it has to be more difficult to sell. Weirdly enough, nine out of ten people I know will say how they find it easier to sell high-ticket than they do lower and I used to be one of those people.

I used to find selling low-ticket really hard. Give me something priced five, six or seven figures and I could do it with my eyes closed, it felt so easy… but low-ticket used to feel like banging my head against a brick wall. In reality, low-ticket isn't any more difficult than high-ticket. It was purely a belief I held because I believed that selling low-ticket meant having to convince people or working harder for less money.

In the same way that people think selling high-ticket is harder because the amount is more, they also think it means that you have to convince people more, you have to justify the figure more, or it's just more difficult because you're asking people to pay more.

Of course, the other aspect to selling high-ticket with ease is the fact you may be sat there wondering if people actually willingly pay these prices and do it with ease. Are there people out there that really pay five, six and seven figures, and they do it with ease?

The answer is, of course, yes, there are people right across the world that are buying at all sorts of levels every single day. Every minute of every day there is big ticket sales being made.

A higher price tag doesn't mean that the selling of it has to be more difficult. You could actually argue the opposite to be the case. As long as you're selling to the right people and your positioning is bang on (we'll get to that in following chapters) then selling can be just as easy no matter what level you're selling at.

I had just finished putting together a six figure offer with a client and we got to the part about selling it and almost immediately she jumped to the idea that selling this would be difficult. I asked her why and she said, "Well, because it's over 100k, it's a lot of money," and of course she was correct - it's not a small amount… but to the right person it's going to be perfect.

This client had recently gone and purchased a very high-end car and paid way more than the price tag for this offer. I asked her whether she thought the person who had sold it to her would have said that the sale was "hard". She replied, "Of course not, I knew I wanted it and I bought it. I'd say it was really easy, actually."

So what's the difference? What was the difference between her going and spending over 100k on something she wanted and the sale being easy versus her selling this? Let's keep in mind she was only going to be selling it to people who would want it, her positioning was bang on and she was already selling high five figures with ease.

The difference was purely the belief she had around it. She believed that selling something worth six figures was going to be hard, because it's a big number, because she'd have to really convince people it was worth it. It was just a belief she held.

She wasn't having to convince people to buy her high five figure offers: why would she have to now? She found selling her high five figures the easiest thing ever: why would she not have the experience now? She herself regularly spent six figures on things she wanted and was the easiest sale, so why wouldn't she see the same in return?

Ultimately it was down to the beliefs she held, the expectations she had and the preconceived ideas she had about selling at different levels.

I could share similar stories for every level of selling. People have the exact same thoughts when they first think about selling 10k, 20k or even higher. The reality is genuinely very different; selling at a higher level does not mean that the sales cannot be as easy as if you sell low-ticket and like I said, there are people out there that would tell you selling high is actually easier than selling low. I used to be one!

The only thing that changes is the number of numbers and your belief around it, the beliefs you have attached to the number. The actual selling part remains the same. Do you have what someone wants? Yes. Do they know about it? Yes. Can they buy it? Yes. Then they'll buy.

And if you're wanting proof (because I know some of you will be thinking it), if you look hard enough you'll find someone in your industry, in your sector, selling the same if not similar to you, selling at what you might think of as eye watering amounts and making the sales with total ease!

Action points

Why do you believe sales has to be hard and what proof do you have to back that up?

How could you allow sales to be easier for you?

Who do you know that's making sales with total ease that can act as proof against your beliefs of sales not being easy?

Chapter Five

LOVE = EFFORTLESS SELLING

*Y*ou might see 'love' and 'sales' next to each other and wonder if I've lost the plot. I haven't and there's actual real logic behind it, which I am of course going to share with you. I'm not about to leave you hanging.

I've spoken previously about selling being of service. Now I'm going to take things a step further and say that selling is sharing the love and love has a massive impact on making sales effortlessly.

We're talking love from various angles: loving sales, loving what you sell, loving how you sell it, loving how you deliver it. Love is one of the key factors in making sales, because the very fact is that if you don't love what you sell, if you don't love how you're selling, if you don't love how you're delivering and if you don't see selling as something you love, then guess what's going to happen?

You'll either not make sales or you'll find that selling is one of the hardest and most frustrating things you'll do. You may find that no matter what you seem to sell it's always an uphill battle to get anyone to buy. You may even actively try and avoid it.

But why?

It's simple. When you have that feeling of love, of excitement, you radiate in a way that you don't otherwise and people feed off that.

Believe it or not, someone on the other end of a phone who can't see you can actually feel when you're smiling, because when you smile your energy changes and they can feel that even if they can't see it. So it stands to reason that the more in love you are with what you're selling, how you sell it, how you deliver it and how you see selling, the bigger the impact is on how easily you find it to make sales.

I've spoken before about the fact that emotion is a large factor in people buying and doing so with ease, so imagine if the emotion you bring to the table is a negative one? Or one that isn't filled with joy? One that isn't 'YESSSS'?

What effect might that have? A negative one obviously, because they will likely feed off your energy. Your energy will have a direct impact on the person you're speaking to. If you're in a space of love they'll feel that, if you're passionate then they'll feel it, if you're excited then they'll feel it. If you're the opposite of all those things, they'll feel that too and it's more likely to cause them to slip into the same energy space, which then of course results in a situation where the sale feels hard.

They're not excited because you're not. Fear has a bigger voice and doubt can come out to play in a bigger way. All this ultimately results in you having that pulling teeth feeling when making sales, which is of course what you don't want, hence why you're reading this book.

Love and selling are directly connected and yet for the most part we're conditioned to see them as things that cannot go together, when in reality the opposite is true. Love and selling are intertwined and connected in ways you may not have considered before. It goes deeper than selling something you love, although this is of course important and we'll talk about it, but I'm talking loving sales as a whole, every single part of it.

Selling isn't a separate thing!

But it is, no?

Isn't selling something separate, away from everything else you do? People will say they love everything about what they do right up until they sell, because selling is seen as this thing that happens away from everything else, separately from it all; it's seen as the big bad wolf where you take people's money.

I've previously covered how selling is actually being of service, but let's talk about why selling is not separate from anything else that you do and why selling is directly connected to what you love.

Selling is something you're doing from the very first moment someone sees or comes across you, from the very first message, because selling isn't just the act of saying "you can buy this"; selling is selling your message, your idea, your passion, your expertise, your services, and yourself, and it happens from the very first second someone enters your world.

The content that you love is already selling. The conversations you have are already selling. The videos you do are already selling. Every single action is selling, because every single action builds up to the point where the actual sale can happen. Why see selling as something that happens separately from everything else? Why disconnect selling from the love you have for everything else that you do?

We've covered how selling is being of service, but selling is also an extension of your passion. It's only with selling that you can reach your full potential with your passion. For example, let's say your passion was helping people get organised with their finances. That's not necessarily going to happen for them without you. The passion you have for helping people do that isn't going to happen for them until they purchase your services.

We all know they could take all of your free content that you put out there with love and passion to help people, and not make a single change. They might not really get the exact help they need with any of that content, but you put it out there with love because it's sharing something you're passionate about - but when it comes to selling people often detach from that same feeling and emotion.

The emotion, love and passion you have for what you're out there sharing to the world is changed when it comes to the actual selling element. It's detached, it's set aside because selling isn't something you can love? It's you taking money from someone.

I disagree. Selling is an extension of everything you're already doing. You are already selling from the very first minute anyone ever joins your audience, your world, reads your content, etc. It's in the selling where you actually get to reach the full potential of your passion, where you get to put that passion out into the world and see it come to life. That doesn't happen to its full potential without selling.

Selling is the vehicle that enables you to take your passion and have it felt by the people who need it, experienced by the right people and impact the world. Without selling, your passion is not truly fulfilled or experienced, it's not truly complete as such. There's only ever so much anyone can do with free words.

If you love what you do, why can't you love the part where the true transformation, your true passion, can be seen, felt and heard? It's connected. It's intertwined. Without selling it simply doesn't ever reach its full potential.

Selling is not something to be embarrassed about, to hide away, be ashamed of. No matter what it is you do, you deserve to be able to sell it. It's in the selling that you'll truly make that difference you desire to make after all.

You can love sales. You can bring that love into your selling, into your process, into your thinking because you've been selling with love from the minute you showed up for the first time or created your first piece of content. You've already been selling whilst loving it.

Selling happens through the whole process and not just in the end piece.

Selling is an extension of your passion. It's where your passion really gets to come to life. It's through selling that you get to reach that full passion potential, and not just for you but for those you desire to work with too.

Selling is not a separate act. You're already selling with love; you're already doing it! See it as an extension: hold that same level of love at every stage of selling.

I'm one of the lucky ones, but I don't recommend it if we're talking effortless selling!

I'm one of those people who can sell anything no matter whether I love it or not, so I'm not about to tell you that you cannot ever sell something you don't love, because that would be a lie. I have spent years selling things I didn't love in any way, shape or form. They were a means to an end, and honestly, I didn't think I had any other options at the time.

You could be the same. You too could be someone who can sell something even if you don't love it, but I don't recommend it. Also, whilst I could make sales selling anything, effortless they were not!

They felt like some of the hardest sales I've ever done, banging my head against what felt like a brick wall only to eventually get the yes. I thought I felt excited for the next few hours only to realise that actually it was relief and then that feeling would soon pass as I realised that now the sale was done it was about delivering something I didn't much care for either. Whilst, sure, you can get away with selling something you don't really love, is that actually what you want? Do you want to be selling something you don't love?

Whilst selling something you don't love is entirely possible, selling something you do love comes with all sorts of perks that I highly recommend.

I consider myself to be extremely blessed, not in the cheesy way, but I'm a part of a small percentage of the population who can hand on heart say they get to spend their days doing something they love. I love what I do, I love all my businesses, I love what I sell, how I deliver it, and how I sell it.

I sit there sometimes and think, *what the actual fuck?* How can living your life doing what you love be something that the vast majority of the population won't experience? Even worse than that is when you consider that there's a large percentage of business owners out there selling things they don't even love!

I mean, what in the actual hell!

Most people become business owners for freedom, to be in charge of their own destiny, to make a difference, to follow a passion, and yet many find themselves selling things they don't even like let alone love. Maybe it's because they think that it's the only way they can make sales or a multitude of other reasons, but whatever it is, I'm here to tell you that it doesn't have to be that way.

If you're one of those people that are selling something they don't love, this is your message, your invitation to stop. To stop selling something because it's what you think you have to do. To stop selling it because you think it's the only option available for you. I'm living proof that isn't the case. I walked away from a highly successful business and have built something even bigger and even more successful whilst doing something I love.

Want to know something really mind blowing? Making 100k, a million even, is actually really easy. It's pretty simple when you break it down. It's just numbers and broken down they're not even that big numbers. And it's not difficult. If it feels difficult then it's likely because you're making it so. You could make 100k, a million, and way more in one of a million different sectors, selling a million different services, doing a million different things. Just look around at all the people who are killing it, making those sales and much more, spread right across the world. You'll find that there are people in every single sector, selling all sorts of different things doing just that!

So why can't you? Why can't you make what you desire whilst selling something you really love?

If I can, if they can, then why can't you?

And why in the fucking hell do you not want to? That sounds really harsh, I know, but why wouldn't you want to?

Given the fact that you can make sales selling absolutely anything these days - you can make 100k by teaching someone how to use a broom (this is a true story by the way!) - why wouldn't you choose to make money doing something you actually love?

Aside from the fact that it's a waste if you don't, it makes the task of making sales so much easier. It's the space where they flow to you, where it feels as if you've just made that sale so easy you didn't even have to try.

Like magic they just flow to you.

Selling something you love is like a magic wand. Why? Simple. The more you love something and the more passion you have for it, the more that radiates out and the more the person you are speaking to, connecting with or being seen by can feel it. Their emotion connects in with yours. If your emotion is a positive, excited, loving, passion-filled one then they will feel into that. They'll feed off that, and they'll be in a space where they cannot wait to say YES!

Your excitement excites them. Your passion fills and fuels them.

But remember, you're not a robot!

I know, sometimes it feels as if it would be easier if we were, but we're not and that's more than ok. However, some of us still operate from the space as if we were.

We set things up or plan things out and then think that's how it should look at every point in the year. I know for me that isn't the case.

I love and crave different things at different times in the year. In the summer I am way more energised than in the winter. I am a Summer person; I love the sun and the heat, hence why I moved to an island where it's summer all year around!

But I'm going to love selling something different in the summer versus the winter. In the winter I actually need something different from the summer. I am fuelled by different things; I am lit up by different things. So my energy around selling different things is also different.

This is something I know in advance because I've taken the time to look at it. When I'm thinking of what to sell, one of the first things I consider is, "What will I love to deliver at that time?"

If I am not going to be delivering something that is right for me, I'm not going to love it and if I'm not going to love it, I'm not going to love selling it: you get the idea here. I've done the whole selling things because I thought I had to or because it was just a means to an end. I spent years doing it and I walked away from it because I wanted to live a limitless life. To me, limitless also includes only selling what I actually want to deliver.

Now you may be reading this and thinking, "That's all well and good but it has to be something people want to buy. Of course it does. There's a difference between selling something you love that other people want to buy versus selling something you love that no one else wants.

Of course you have to be selling something that others want, but that's to do with how you position what you're selling, and maybe the topic of what you're selling too. You can position anything to hit your ideal clients in the way that gets them to say, "I need that," or, "I want that." It all comes down to your positioning of something. It's always going to be an easier sell when you have something positioned right but also when it is something you want to actually deliver or provide.

I love helping people make high-ticket sales. Sometimes I love delivering that with in-person events, yet other times of the year delivering an in-person event is my idea of hell! I understand the concept that I am not the same all of the time. I am not always fuelled in the same way 365 days a year. What fuels me, what lights me up, changes and so naturally I change what I sell accordingly. You may be very different from me in this aspect, and if you are then that's awesome, but if you're similar to me then ensuring you're selling what you love at the times that are right for you through the year is important.

We already know I break the mould in many ways. I wouldn't, for example, say that I am going to launch something and sell it in February because everyone else is. First of all, the idea of piling in and launching something at the same time of the year, the same as everyone else, just a different topic, is completely my idea of hell. I'd procrastinate on it so much to ensure I missed all of the deadlines so I wouldn't sell it, because it would be that out of alignment for me.

But I speak to people who do, because they think the only time they can sell is that time because, well… that's what other people say. Other people also say that the earth is flat... but let's be very clear here, that's not the case!

Similarly, it's not the case that you can't make just as much sales or even more if you sold something at a different time of year. That one window other people use to sell that one style of thing isn't the only window, it's just their window and often everyone follows, but does that mean you have to?

If it felt right for you, if it was genuinely something you wanted to do then I say go for it. But if it's not, please don't. You are far more likely to see better sales results and feel better about all of the sales you do make and make those sales easier, if you're selling the right thing for you at the right time.

I'm going to say this really loud and clear so everyone in the back can hear me... you can sell high-ticket (or anything) at any time of the year and make a shed load of sales whilst doing it! Don't be dictated to. You will always find making sales easier, more effortless and more fun when you're selling something you love at a time that's also aligned for you.

Delivery also matters!

It's a common belief that when selling high-ticket you only have one option - one to one and that's it. Well, we already know that's not the case as I've already spoken about it in this book, and yet it's still something that the vast majority of people do believe.

It often results in people selling something they don't actually love. When thinking about doing what you love it's easy to put the focus on the topic of what you're selling or the service you're providing, but what about delivery?

You have a choice!

You have a choice as to how you deliver something. Just because you're selling something high-ticket doesn't mean you're stuck with one option. Even if you're a website designer providing a service, you are still not stuck having to deliver in just one way. There are so many options as to how you can deliver something and it's important that you're delivering in a way you love.

Just like all the other aspects of selling what you love that we've covered, it's equally important to be delivering in a way that you love. If you're going to spend any amount of time, whether it be an hour or ten months, delivering something, it needs to be something you actually want to do.

Contrary to what you might think or see the vast majority of time online, you do have more than one option.

Just because you might be a coach, it doesn't mean the only high-ticket you can ever deliver is a one to one. Just because you're a website designer, it doesn't mean your only option is to deliver this six week 'done for you' service.

Whatever it is you do, you have options and high-ticket actually gives you more options than any other model out there.

It can be moulded and flexed into anything you desire. You can deliver anything from hybrids, events, one to one, group, courses, retreats… the list goes on. You can even take two or three of those and combine them to create a delivery experience that's perfect for you.

We can spend so much time thinking about all the other aspects of our business and yet the delivery of something is often forgotten about, because, well… everyone else just does this or I see everyone doing this so it must mean I have to deliver it in the same way.

But I can almost guarantee you there is someone out there in every sector providing a service that looks a little different, delivering in a way that's not the same as everyone else.

One of the very reasons I love helping people sell high-ticket is because I know just how flexible it can be. I know that no matter what their vision, no matter what they love, they can leverage high-ticket to bring that vision to life. Whether they never want to work one to one with someone or whether they want to travel the world working one to one with people, it's all possible.

The most important thing ultimately is that they're delivering in a way they love - that *you* deliver in a way that you love. It may be something you haven't even considered or you may have fallen into the trap of thinking that even though you love delivering in one way you have to have other options – that there have to be other ways of delivering because otherwise you won't have a proper business or it'll feel like you're doing something wrong.

Is that really true though?

I know people who only work and deliver their services one way. I'm really not a fan of online courses. I certainly don't like delivering them and I like selling them even less. I'll be honest and say I had previously fallen into the trap of thinking I needed them; I mean, other people who were at the level I then desired to be at were all selling them so I had to, right?

I thought it would be the only way to sell seven figures, the only way to have six figure months and more. The only way I could ever possibly scale. So I tried it and just like the first time I tried selling them, I hated it. Not because I couldn't sell though, I could have sold them and a lot of them if I'd really wanted to, but not at any point did it light me up, not in any way, shape or form, and being honest, they were only there to fill a hole I had told myself I needed to fill.

I didn't need them. I've since scaled way past where I was originally intending online courses to take me and I did it without focusing on them. I've continued to have them available on my website but I haven't launched one in years. Despite it being something that so many others preach you have to have, the only way to unlock time freedom, I've managed all of that and more without focusing on them, without selling them.

There is always more than one way, and I would choose the way that involves me loving what I am doing, delivering and selling over going through the motions or doing it because I believe that's what I have to do, every single day of the week, ten lifetimes over.

If you're looking for permission or looking for proof that you can do something different, that you can take what you love, deliver it in a way that you love, deliver it in a way that's different from others, *and* still achieve what you desire, still have time freedom and still make sales with ease... then here it is and here I am!

Before you decide how to deliver something in the future, before you fall into the trap of thinking it has to look a certain way because that's what everyone else does, check in with yourself and ask yourself how you would love to deliver it to provide the service or whatever it is you sell.

Loving what you sell, loving sales and how you deliver it is by far one of the most important aspects of selling effortlessly!

We can't talk about loving sales and not cover this final piece of the love aspect

The final piece in our love fest (I just wanted to slide that in there, to be honest) is who you're selling to.

Now this might seem the most logical. After all, we're always told to work with people we actually love working with, right? It's something we see everywhere and yet a large percentage of us don't look at the bigger picture of what that means.

A large number of people just think of it as being something like, is the person nice? Yes. Do they want what I'm selling? Yes. Great, then they're my people and I should sell to them.

But if we're talking selling to those we're going to love working with, then actually we want to look a little deeper than that. Because what we're also talking about is the person you're going to potentially be spending time with, vibing with, delivering to.

That person isn't just a tick box of "do they need what I'm selling" or "they seem nice", it's about the person as a whole. It's not thinking about this from an ideal client point of view, we're thinking about this from a people to people type of view.

I don't know about you, but I don't vibe with everyone. There are some people that seem to rub me up the wrong way without them even doing anything. They're just not my people, and I'm not theirs. The thing is, in the past I did actually end up working with them too. I didn't think of selling to those you'll love to work with as anything deeper than a tick box, and who was I to say no or not sell something to someone just because I didn't really vibe with them?

The real question should have been, who am I *not*? I can assure you of one thing, had I not sold to them, had I had a boundary of not working with those I wouldn't love to work with, I'd have not just saved myself time and them time, but it would also have made for a much better experience all around.

Those sales are always some of the hardest. I didn't even really want to sell to them and yet I did anyway because I felt I had to. I felt it would be wrong not to, given that they needed and wanted my help.

But I didn't feel lit up when I made the sale. The sales were some of the hardest I've ever made. I dreaded every time I was going to speak to them. I even dreaded seeing their names come up in my emails.

From start to finish, nothing about the experience brought me joy, and quite frankly I was debating what the hell I was doing. I may as well have just stayed in my last business if I was going to end up doing things and working with people I didn't like!

So I stopped thinking about who was I not to allow someone to buy from me and work with me, and instead started to think about who was I *not*?

When I thought about it, by allowing them to buy from me even though I knew I probably wouldn't enjoy it all that much, I was doing the opposite of what I wanted to do. I wasn't being fully of service, I wasn't operating from a space of love and I was not providing a great experience for either party.

I dived into thinking about who I love to work with, who I *really* love to work with, and who if I could have ten million of I'd love every minute of it. Then I set up boundaries that meant they were the only people I'd work with, the only people I'd even consider selling to.

These days I turn down more requests to work with me than I accept, not because I couldn't help them but because it wouldn't be an enjoyable experience for me. They're not my people and in turn that would make it a not very enjoyable experience for them. So I don't sell to them, they don't work with me and I don't filter myself either. This means that if someone who isn't for me sees my content, they're going to know they don't vibe with me.

Even on the homepage of my website I make it quite clear who I am for and who I'm not for, and I don't apologise for it.

If you're selling to people you don't love working with, you're going to hate it. It's going to feel hard and you might even hold yourself back from making sales because you don't want to put yourself in the position of working with people you don't enjoy working with. When you filter people out, when you decide not to say yes to everyone, and when you have clear boundaries of who you do or don't work with, you are being of service, not just to you but to the people you're saying no to.

It can seem like an odd concept that saying no to someone is actually being of service, but it is, because forging ahead would make for a not very enjoyable experience with you and if you don't enjoy it, your energy will show it!

"A limitless life isn't just about unlocking time freedom or financial freedom, it's about being in alignment with how you unlock it too!"

Action points:

What do you actually love to do?

How do you love to deliver and work?

Are there times of the year when you crave different things?

What would being in alignment with what you're selling look like and mean for you?

Chapter Six

I AM NOT YOU AND YOU ARE NOT ME!

When people think of making sales they often jump to the same conclusions. We see successful people in our feed every day and so when we're thinking about making sales of our own we often assume that's exactly how we have to do it as well.

If they do sales calls, I have to. If they do webinars, I have to. If they do ads, I have to. If they do sales pages, I have to. If they do messages, I have to.

I know I did that. The weird thing is that I ignored everything I once did or knew about selling in my first business and instead fell into this trap of thinking I had to sell this specific way.

In my case I believed the ONLY way I could make sales online was to follow this process: webinar > book loads of calls in > sale.

I lost count of the number of webinars I did and I hated every single one. I'm not a webinar gal at all and yet I was trying to sell using them and everything I actually knew about calls, and I was still throwing it all out of the window and trying to force a system I didn't feel aligned with at all.

Then there were those endless funnels constantly selling someone into something else. That's not my idea of high-ticket selling and quite frankly turns me right off!

Want to know what happened when I followed all of these golden sales strategies that were totally out of alignment for me? Nothing, that's what happened! I was so out of alignment that I hated it all, and of course showing up with that energy is never the right approach. Worse than that, I ended up attracting everyone under the sun that was not a good fit to work with me.

I thought I wasn't cut out for this online stuff after all. Maybe I should go back to creating a different type of business because I could smash sales out of the park back then. I actually considered doing just that until I had an AHA moment when I realised I didn't need to go back. I just needed to harness my own power and sell in a way that was right for me and also right for those I actually wanted to work with.

I went from no sales when trying to sell in a way that was aligned for someone else to making over 100k cash sales in under six months by harnessing what was in alignment for me.

It's one of my biggest bugbears with selling - everyone thinks there's just one way to do it or that you just have to copy how someone else is selling. Sure, being inspired by how they're selling is good and if it's in alignment for you, then awesome, but the real key to making sales feel totally effortless is selling in a way that's in alignment for you. Being in alignment really matters. You might think it doesn't but it does.

When you try to sell in a way that doesn't fit for you, what happens?

Well, a few things can happen. First of all, you may not want to do it in the first place so you might not take the action. Secondly, you might end up in a situation where like me you attract people who aren't who you want to be working with. Thirdly, you might end up making sales but they sure as shit won't feel effortless.

I know I've said this already, maybe even multiple times. But selling effortlessly and making sales that feel effortless isn't largely down to strategy. In fact strategy plays a much smaller part in it. Making sales that feel really effortless is largely down to you.

How will sales ever feel effortless if you're trying to do it in a way you don't like? Who even made the rule that everyone had to sell in the same way otherwise they wouldn't successfully make sales?

I've spoken to people who believed they couldn't sell in the way they wanted to because it was a masculine way to sell and they're not a man… I mean, WHAT?!

Just because you're a female doesn't mean you can only sell in xyz ways, just like there are plenty of men that can sell using more feminine strategies and approaches and it is in total alignment for them. It's time to stop seeing sales as a one way, one method, one skill and that's the way it has to look. In reality, it really doesn't.

Want to know why those people you look up to are killing it with sales? Because they're in their zone of genius in every single area and that includes how they're selling. I know that I wouldn't sell even half as well as I do right now if I was doing it from anywhere other than a place of total alignment for me. Believe me I have tried.

Do I sell the conventional way like others in my field? No. I probably stand out as one of the few odd ones out that don't "conform" to those strategies and approaches, but those strategies and approaches aren't in alignment with me.

Think of it like this. You may have heard that:

You have to use sales pages - I barely use sales pages. I have them created and use them when my team reminds me or I just put them on the website. Other than that I barely use them and I regularly sell out my offers without one.

You have to do webinars - I hate them... the end! I genuinely do not like them so I don't do them. Period.

You have to do sales calls - No sales calls is my default. If you're interested in working with me on any of my offers that are less than 10k then I don't do calls at all. But for all of my offers, no sales call is the default.

You have to have a full photo shoot - Until I moved to Lanzarote in 2019 I never bothered with one and yet I was selling out my high-ticket offers for three years before that.

You have to make sure they make a decision there and then - I'm not bothered. If they want to go away and talk it over with someone, they're more than welcome; if they want to go away and think about it, they're welcome to do that too. I don't need to hold on to the sale or have them say yes right then. I know they'll come back!

You have to get them to hand over their credit card details right away - Umm, no and that's before we've even got into whether they actually have the correct systems and policies that enable them to even do that.

You've got to sell to thousands otherwise you'll never scale - Not my style. I've made millions selling high-ticket whilst continuing to serve in a way that's right for me. You can scale in a million different ways.

I could keep that list going on, but despite ticking pretty much every box of what someone else swears by I still smash my sales out and sell so easily that half the time I don't even feel like I've "sold" in ages.

Despite not doing any of that I've still made millions in sales. I've still consistently sold out my offers. I've still got a waitlist. I've still achieved all these amazing things people aspire to achieve - but I've done it in my own way.

I sell in a way that's right for me and you should too. I don't want you to read this book and think, "I just need to sell like Jane." No you don't, you need to sell like YOU!

I want you to read this book, walk away and be empowered to sell in a way that is in alignment for you. That may well be endless funnels and sales calls. If it is, then amazing, but if it isn't, please stop forcing yourself to do it.

Everyone always says, "But I don't know how to sell." In reality everyone does, it's just they think they have to sell like someone else is selling and that's when they think, "Well, I can't do that," or they see selling as this skill that they don't know, or as we covered before they're missing some magic word to say on a sales call.

You do know how to sell, but you know how to do it in your way. This book isn't about helping you follow how I sell. I mean, if how I sell is in alignment for you then perfect, but I'm never about creating cookie cutter people. I could line my clients up in a row and they'd all sell in slightly different ways and some of them sell in very different ways from me.

That's a large part of selling effortlessly, doing so in YOUR way!

Not mine. Not that other person's. Not that other expert's. Yours.

The way that feels so natural to you, the way that lights you up, the way that doesn't have you cringing or wishing the ground would swallow you whole, that doesn't have you sitting there going, "please no!"

Whilst you could potentially make sales that way, would they be effortless? Doubtful. Would you love it? No. Would you feel lit up and energised by your selling? No. And why would you want that for yourself?

We'll often talk about freedom: time freedom, financial freedom, freedom to travel, etc. etc., but many of us still see sales as something that just *is*.

Many of us think it can't be part of the freedom other than the thing that enables you to open the door to that freedom, but I see it differently. I'm all about living limitlessly but that means in all areas and that includes how you're making it happen.

It's selling in a way that makes you feel as limitless as the time freedom you'll be unlocking. It's selling in a way that makes you feel as limitless as the full bank account will.

It's not accepting that you don't feel very limitless where you are, but it's ok because the money will make you feel better. NO!

It's time we all stopped doing that. It doesn't have to be one or another; it doesn't have to be that you sacrifice your one feeling here to get more of another feeling somewhere else. You can love sales and you can feel as limitless about selling as you do about anything else, but you have to do it in a way that's right for you.

I think it's worth noting that times are changing too. People are becoming wise to those sales tactics and strategies that have been waved around as being the golden answer to everyone making sales. They're growing tired of the endless funnels, the free calls that are actually sales calls, the webinars that are fifty minutes of pitching and ten minutes of value, the sales processes that are the same for everyone, so similar you can predict what's coming next.

People are growing tired of it: they want something more, something more real, something that's more aligned with them as individuals and also enables them to really connect in and vibe more with the person they're looking to buy from.

Finding your own way to sell that is in alignment with you is 100% the future!

I am not always the same and neither are you.

This might come as a surprise to you but I don't always sell in the same way. Sometimes I sell an offer very differently from how I sold it before. Why? Because sometimes I change!

I know - shock horror - but I feel differently about how I sell some offers compared with how I sell others. Some might say I even feel called in different ways to different offers. The fact is, I am not a one size fits all person.

I change and you likely do as well. I even change with the seasons. I'm a much happier, brighter person in the summer, that's for sure!

A side issue I see with selling is that we put ourselves into a box that says, 'ok this is how it must always look.'

But why?

Do you belong in a box? Is your life always the same? Do you always feel the same? No, just like the seasons change, how you choose to sell can change too.

When selling one offer you might feel way more called to sell in a different way than before and you know what - that's OK!

You're not wrong. You're not weird. You're not a failure. You're not bad at business. You're a human and sometimes we feel called or more aligned to do something in a slightly different way.

It boggles my brain sometimes how we accept that so many things can change, we'll happily accept that things can be adjusted or look slightly different sometimes, but when it comes to selling and the way you sell, for so many people it's just, "this is the box and this is how it must always look."

Why?

It doesn't have to actually look like that at all. I didn't get into business to be stuck in the same box month after month and never be allowed to change it.

I got into business to make my own rules. To be in control of how I wanted things to look. To not have to follow other people's stupid ways of doing things. To be able to feel a level of freedom that a large percentage of the population will never get to experience. And that for me includes being able to change how I want to do something, to be able to change how I choose to approach something, to change based upon what it is that I'm actually selling.

Something I always say to my clients is that they make the rules, not me, not anyone else but themselves. If they want to change how they sell, they can. If they want to sell one offer differently from another, they can. If they want to do whatever the hell they want to do... they can.

Because they make the rules. You make the rules.

The space where you'll make sales effortlessly is always going to be the space in which you are in alignment;

what alignment looks like for you might depend on the time of year, the thing that you're selling or something else. Give yourself permission to sell in different ways if you feel called to. Don't stick yourself in a box and say, "This is the only way I can ever sell."

Uncomfortable doesn't mean you have to push through anyway

I once had a new client who sent me a message in tears. She was trying to do something that took her right out of alignment with how she wanted to sell. She spent hours upon hours trying to do this thing, had procrastinated on it for most of the day and ended up in a voice note to me in tears.

She said to me, "Please don't tell me I have to do this. Is there any other way?"

Without even a single thought, I replied and said, "Stop. Step away from it, throw it away." I'd never tell her that she had to do it this way and I was a little puzzled as to why she thought of doing it this way anyway - I knew it wasn't in alignment for her.

What had happened was pretty simple. She had seen posts and content from other people basically saying that unless you do xyz you'll never make sales. Before she knew it she had taken herself down a path that was so out of alignment for her it was insane. Not only did it make her feel extremely uncomfortable but it had her in a place where she just couldn't focus. It was so out of alignment that it was going to cause her to freeze and not even get the thing out there that she wanted to sell in the first place.

Instead of forcing her forward out of alignment, we threw it to the side and we explored how she'd love to sell it. How did she imagine herself selling it? How would she enjoy selling it? In what way would it feel amazing to sell it?

And from there we built out a sales strategy that was in alignment for her, one that still made her feel a little uncomfortable (because she was still working through sales beliefs as we all do) but one that underneath the fear did excite her.

She went on to sell out every single space. It was, in her own words, the easiest 90k she had ever made and since then she has harnessed selling in her own way to grow a multiple seven figure business. She's come a long way from that voice note in total tears, trying to force herself to sell in a way that wasn't right for her.

The thing is, we've been told often enough that success isn't found in your comfort zone, that sometimes we have to make sacrifices or do things that are uncomfortable for us, otherwise we won't grow and we won't see the results we desire.

To a certain degree I agree but in other ways I don't.

Do you remember in school, how we'd all be told to stand up in front of the class and give a presentation on something? Well, I hated it; I absolutely dreaded it.

And the feedback was always the same. Just talk louder. Just smile more. Just talk about this.

But every time I'd say how much I hated or dreaded it, I'd just be told that it's normal to feel uncomfortable and I had to push through. Eventually I wouldn't be afraid of public speaking, as they put it.

I left school still feeling the same way. In fact, I'd say it wasn't until this year that I have got comfortable with public speaking. I'm still nervous about doing it, but nowhere near the space I was before where I'd burst into tears and feel so sick I couldn't think.

I only got to this space after working with a public speaking coach who understood me. It wasn't about forcing me to go up on that stage in a way that wasn't right for me. It wasn't about forcing me to become someone different, talk about something I didn't enjoy, make me dress a certain way, or in fact say anything I was uncomfortable with.

It was about helping me step into a place where despite the nerves I was actually inspired and excited to get up there and talk, to have a talk that played to my strengths, a talk that enabled me to showcase who I was, and a message that meant it was important I stood up as me and not someone else.

It was about thinking of things I could do to help ease those nerves a little before going on stage that were right for me. Not things that everyone else did so that had to be what I do. Things that would actually help me.

I feel differently about public speaking now because it is set up in a way that is right for me. I still feel nervous over it and a little uncomfortable but there's a difference between now and how I used to feel. The key difference is that I am now in alignment whereas I wasn't before.

This is how I think of the sales aspect. It is completely and entirely normal to feel nervous, to feel a little uncomfortable. I've lost count of the number of messages I get about feeling sick before they post something, send a message, do a video, do a call. But that's just because they're a little nervous, and when they've done it that feeling is gone and they feel amazing!

Should you be forcing yourself into selling in a way that makes you feel so uncomfortable and out of alignment? No. Never. Period. It's not a case of, "You just have to suck it up and get over it." It's not, "It's tough, it's just something you have to learn."

Sure you'll feel a little nervous. You might feel sick. You might feel a little worried. But that's ok, because deep down you'll still have a feeling of excitement. You'll still feel as if this might be uncomfortable a little but that's ok.

Selling in a different way because the other way makes you feel so uncomfortable does not mean you're a failure or chickening out or not a serious business owner. All it means is that you're choosing to sell in alignment versus not. It's in that space that you'll not just see more sales, not just makes sales easier, but you'll feel so free in doing so!

The flip side is you could force yourself to push through, force yourself to conform, force yourself to do it anyway even though you hate it, even though it feels so ridiculously uncomfortable and you cannot stand it. In the end you might make a few sales, but will they ever feel as easy? No.

Will they ever feel like they flow? No. Will they ever light you up? No. Will you ever truly feel freedom? No.

There's a big difference between feeling uncomfortable with something because you just haven't done it before and you're nervous versus feeling so uncomfortable you hate the idea of what you feel you have to do.

No matter what your fear might say. No matter what you might see others say. No matter what that bloody quote on Instagram says.

You don't ever have to force yourself to implement a strategy that is totally out of alignment for you just to make the sales you desire and certainly not to reach the success you desire either.

If you take nothing else away from this book just take this away... YOU make the rules, YOU are always in charge of what's right for you and YOU are always the superpower to achieving all the sales you ever desire. All you ever have to do is align with it!

Action points:

The first part is always getting to know yourself. If you close your eyes and imagine yourself effortlessly selling, what does that look like?

Think about things like:

How would I love to receive sales and new clients?

How do I love being sold to?

Is there an experience where I was sold to that I truly enjoyed and felt easy?

What does effortless selling look like for me?

Explore you, explore what lights you up, explore how you'd really love to make sales!

As a small side note, explore from the space you desire to be in and don't worry about the how just yet. Don't worry about how you'd find people to buy in this way or how you'd create a strategy that would enable you to sell like this. Just focus on letting your imagination explore what you truly feel aligned with. We can get to the rest later.

Chapter Seven

BUYING ISN'T ONE SIZE FITS ALL

Have you ever been interested in buying something but didn't follow through and buy it?

I know I have, many times and not always because of price. Sometimes I didn't follow through and buy it because I didn't know what the price was to begin with and I'm not the type of person that goes any further with something if I don't know the price.

I'm that type of buyer that likes to see all of the information in front of me, where I can just click and buy. I don't want to have to jump through a million hoops, I don't want to have to go on a treasure hunt to find things out and I certainly don't want to have to spend an hour of my time on a call to find any of this out or be able to buy.

The thing is, though, there are people that are the total opposite to that. For everything I hate, others love; for everything I love, others hate.

Just like you may like to sell in a different way, people like to buy in different ways. It's why I'm massively against the whole cookie cutter sales approaches. There is not a one size fits all in this scenario. How your audience might like to buy is completely different to mine. Yours may like to spend ages reading a ton of information. Mine might scroll to the end of the page to the price. Yours may like to browse the long sales pages. Mine might never get to the sales page and prefer to buy immediately off a video.

Imagine you have a sales process and strategy that is the exact opposite of how your ideal clients actually like to buy. What do you think is going to happen?

In general it will be one of three things:

1. You'll attract the wrong people who aren't actually your ideal clients
2. You'll feel as if every sale is pulling teeth and anything but ease and flow
3. You won't make any sales at all

Now you don't want any of those, right?

Of course you don't. If you did you wouldn't be reading about making high-ticket sales (or any sales for that matter) with ease.

Having a sales process that fits your ideal clients perfectly is highly important when it comes to effortlessly selling high-ticket. Think about the sales process as a journey for your ideal clients, the ones you want to be working with, the ones who cannot wait to buy from you. The experience begins in your sales process. Now imagine if that sales process and experience is the total opposite of how they actually like to experience things. What's the chances of you converting the sale with ease?

You'll essentially be operating against them, which either results in sales feeling hard, no sales at all or attracting in the wrong people as your sales process attracts the people who aren't your ideal clients.

A client of mine came to me with that exact issue. They seemed to attract everyone onto sales calls other than the people they actually wanted to work with and who were ready to invest. They couldn't figure out what they were doing wrong.

They had changed their offers. They had changed their marketing. They had changed absolutely everything. And yet still they kept attracting the wrong person and their calls just weren't converting. They had even spent months in pursuit of that magic sales script which never worked either.

I asked them the question of how their ideal clients actually like to buy? How do they buy from others? How do they typically buy? What would their buying profile be?

A lightbulb moment happened. She realised that her sales process was set up to attract the total opposite of what her ideal clients would want to do.

She didn't display her prices, but when exploring her ideal clients' buying habits and profiles she discovered that actually they only take the next step and buy when they're aware of prices up front.

She discovered a number of other things, but everything was centred around the fact that they loved speed; they loved having all of the information and just being able to buy. Her sales process was set up in the opposite way. Everything was kept a mystery until they got on a call with her.

Just by changing her sales process she went from sales that felt really hard that ended with nightmare clients to actually making sales way easier, in way less time and with the people she dreamed of working with.

Who'd have thought that changing a sales process could make such a difference? But it does.

It makes logical sense when you think about it. There are billions of people on the planet and we're all attracted to different things. We enjoy different experiences: some people would run up to a 30ft diving board and just dive straight off; some others wouldn't ever dare do it, whilst others would cautiously walk to the edge before convincing themselves to jump off.

We enjoy different things. We thrive in different environments. We respond to different things. We are not all the same, so why would we think that we all like to buy in the exact same way?

I know of people who go into those electronic mega stores and love being sold to. I go in and get highly irritated by the person following me around asking me a million questions about budget. I mean, budget?! If I see something I like, I'll buy it. That's when I know what my budget for that item would be.

Others go in, seek someone out, read out their entire list of budget, requirements, get into a chat and allow themselves to be sold every upsell under the sun. That is my idea of hell.

I see what I want and I want it, so let me pay and leave me alone. I'm a nightmare to sell to but if you try selling to me in a way I don't enjoy I won't buy. I will go out of my way to avoid that sales experience; it genuinely doesn't light me up at all.

And you might be thinking, but does a buying experience need to light someone up?

Well, it certainly needs to make them feel excited, comfortable, buzzed, connected, easy... it needs to make them feel a whole host of things if you want to have the conversion and particularly when we're talking in a high-ticket environment.

It also matters because they'll remember it. You remember your terrible buying experiences, right? That's not how you want your ideal clients to feel buying from you. You want them to feel like you feel about *your* positive buying experiences. I'm sure you have them and more than likely they're the ones where you haven't even really felt as if you were sold to. That's because the process was perfect for you, because the buying experience was aligned for you and how you like to buy.

There are these main buyers:

THE ACTION TAKER

They dive in. They see what they want, they know they want it and they want to grab it. Speed is highly important and they don't want to have to wait or jump through a million hoops. They know they want it, so let them have it. They don't really want to browse long sales pages; they just want to be able to buy.

THE MIDDLE OF THE ROAD

They're slightly more cautious than the action taker. They see something they want but they're not going to dive in right away. Sometimes they have some questions but other times they just want to observe a little bit longer, maybe even wait for a sign that tells them they should definitely buy this!

THE CAUTIOUS ONE

They don't impulse buy unless it's something they really, really want and have probably been thinking about for a while. They're likely to spend a lot longer thinking about something before they jump. They tend to need a little bit more encouragement and reassurance before they're ready and willing to take that leap and buy.

Which one do you feel you are? You might be different in different situations, which is also important to know when it comes to your ideal client.

When you think about buying as being an experience, it's an experience that generally speaking we choose. You can see how it plays a part in how easy you feel you make sales. You can see how it translates into you creating a sales process that is set up and in alignment with what your ideal clients would be looking for. You can also see how a sales process that isn't in alignment with that person will result in sales feeling hard or attracting the wrong people into the sales process, in some ways potentially even not making sales at all.

The more you think of your sales process as something that is a buying experience for your ideal clients, the easier your sales will flow. When you think about how they like to buy, when you think about the process they enjoy going through, you can then create a sales environment that results in making those sales effortlessly.

But everyone is in Facebook groups!

Having a sales process that is aligned with how your ideal clients like to buy is also connected with where it is you're showing up to attract leads and potential sales in the first place.

Just like people like to buy in different ways, we don't all hang out in the same place either, and yet it can sometimes feel as if the whole internet is telling you that all you need to do is have a Facebook group and you'll have it full of your people. Because, Facebook has billions of users, right?

That's true, but while my father has a Facebook profile and he is someone's ideal client, you won't get him buying from you on there. He uses it to ring me and see my pictures - that's it. He doesn't scroll his newsfeed. He doesn't join in groups. He has never clicked or looked at an ad. He goes on, calls me or goes to my profile. That is as far as it goes. So if your ideal client was my father, having a Facebook group or even using Facebook in general would be totally lost.

If I was your ideal client you probably wouldn't find me buying from you on LinkedIn. Whilst it's a massively popular platform for many of my clients, I don't hang out there. I have a profile but I don't spend time there and I've never purchased anything from there. That's not to say others don't. Huge numbers of sales and leads are generated via LinkedIn every day but not for everyone.

And that's kind of the point... whether we're talking the sales process itself or where you're showing up to grow your audience and attract leads, it always has to be centred around your ideal clients and not what cookie cutter approach someone else is using.

For every person who makes sales with ease using Facebook groups, you'll find others who never use it. For every person who makes high-ticket sales with their eyes closed on LinkedIn, you'll again find others who never use it. You are always going to have more success, attract the right people and make sales with ease when you're in the right spaces. This isn't to say that Facebook isn't for you - it might well be. I'm not saying LinkedIn isn't for you either. What matters is whether it's right for who you actually want to buy from you.

So many people are just taking someone else's lead generation and sales process, plugging it into their own business and hoping it'll then rain sales because it works so well for that other person, but it works really well for that other person because it's actually right for them and who they sell to.

If you have something that you've plugged in but isn't created for you and isn't set up for the people you want to buy from you, it'll be like pushing water uphill. Instead of sitting there and asking yourself the question about what works really well for others, start thinking about you and who you want to sell to.

Where do they actually hang out?

Where are they buying services similar to yours from?

Where are they already buying from?

How are they using the platforms they are on?

It isn't always the best idea to keep it hidden

I'm talking about that age-old question of whether you should display your price or not. And honestly it comes down to your ideal clients and why you'd be keeping it hidden.

I won't go any further if I don't know the price. I find it incredibly irritating if I can't see the price. If I know I already want something, the price will not put me off. I will still buy, but if the price is hidden - that will put me off.

I could really want something but if I don't see the price I won't go any further, because I don't really have the time to go on a treasure hunt and I certainly don't want to spend an hour or so on a call just to find out the price to then potentially be able to buy.

But as we've already covered, not everyone is like that. There are people who are the complete opposite, who actually prefer the opposite to me and so not having the price would definitely suit them. Sometimes it can work in your favour if you're trying to create an exclusive aspect to your work.

The issue I generally see with this topic is that lots of people aren't displaying the price out of fear or because they've previously been told that you shouldn't put the price because you'll scare people off: keep it until the call and then you can convince them.

I'm totally against that and quite frankly, it's total crap. Why do you even want to spend your time on calls having to convince people to buy from you? That doesn't sound like effortless selling to me, that sounds like a bloody nightmare.

Yet that's exactly what happens for many, maybe even for you. Some people end up scheduling their calendar full of calls with prospects, none of whom know the price, none of whom are really their ideal clients, and they end up spending hours upon hours on these calls trying to convince these people to buy from them only to end up converting none or just one.

What's the purpose of a sales page if you haven't been able to demonstrate the value? If they've made it through your whole sales page and they're interested, why would the price then suddenly put the right person off if the value has been demonstrated, which it should have been if the right person is now excited?

And that's one of the main issues: too many people are just selling to everyone and anyone and they think that someone being scared off by a price is a bad thing. I disagree entirely. I want people to be put off by my pricing because I am not for everyone. Not everyone is even ready to work with me and if they're not there are other options available to them. The price should actually act as a barrier of entry. It should put off those who aren't ready or a right fit yet.

Pricing isn't just a bunch of numbers. It can really help you filter out the wrong people versus the right people. It can filter out those who are ready versus those who are not and if they're not you can always direct them somewhere else. Isnt it better to save them and yourself time and have that filtering out happen before they've got to the end of a sixty minute call with you?

Whether you put the price or not comes down to what's right for your ideal clients, for the sales and buying process, and the experience. It may be that you put the price for some offers and not for others, but there's one thing for certain - you should never not put the price only because you're afraid you'll put people off!

If you're afraid of putting people off, then the question is what do you think you'd be able to do differently on a call that would convince them that the price is good that you can't do anywhere else? Would the people who are put off by price actually buy anyway, even at a much lower price? Even if you did manage to convince them, would that even be an experience you or they would enjoy?

I'm not talking about not dealing with objections. In fact, there's a whole chapter on this later on, but the idea that we have to convince people to want to buy from us is something I just don't buy into. I don't want to spend my time having to convince people. I'm going to talk more about that in the next chapter and why I'm against it. So I'll leave that for now.

Just remember that when it comes to pricing, if your ideal clients are like me, you could potentially be putting us off by not showing the price way more than you ever would by just putting that price out there. Don't ever let fear put you off showing the price; don't let fear convince you that you price is something you should hide. For the right people you don't need to hide it.

It's safe to think outside of the box...

I've talked a lot in this chapter about the buying and sales experience. You might be sat there thinking, "How would I make an experience out of this?" I want to encourage you to think out of the box a little. This might not be relevant or a fit for all of you - remember we've talked about how your ideal clients like to buy and the buying experience *they'd* love to have.

But for some of you this might be really relevant and something you haven't thought of so listen up. When we talk about the experience, that doesn't necessarily just have to include what you might deliver in the way of a sales page or call. It can include something much bigger and more creative!

A client of mine sends out invitations inviting people to work with her in one of her six figure offers. No sales pages, no freebies, none of that. She hand picks who she invites in and then takes them on one amazing sales and buying experience which begins with a personalised invitation which includes gifts. I can't go into a ton of detail, but the process is delivered in a couple of different steps over a couple of weeks, and each step takes them on a journey. She has a 100% conversion with this, for a high six figure offer.

Another client sends something after the initial sales process has begun, so when the initial conversation has happened for that person to become a warm lead they send them something. Unlike the previous client example, this one isn't so much about sending something that takes them on a journey, but rather sending them something that makes the potential client feel extremely special and catered for. This is incredibly important for the type of person that they work with as it's one of the most important aspects when this person is deciding to buy. Creating an experience that has this person feeling really valued and catered for is incredibly important.

I could share a ton of other examples where thinking outside of the box has helped create an amazing sales and buying experience. The reason I'm sharing this is because you can get creative; don't be afraid to think outside of the box. For some of you this might be exactly what you need to do in order to get the YES and work with the people you truly desire to be working with.

The sales isn't just about having a sales page or sales call or a Facebook group even, and I think for a large number of people that's been forgotten. Everyone is consumed with thinking about all of those kinds of things and they forget about the bigger picture. They've forgotten that there's a big wide world out there full of so many different people, and that so many different experiences can be delivered outside of the online things you may see others doing every single day.

There are people offering some of the most unique buying experiences you could ever imagine. You won't see them in your Facebook feed or group doing it because that's not where their ideal clients hang out and that's certainly not the experience their ideal clients crave to buy from. Just because you don't see it doesn't mean you can't do it, and it certainly doesn't mean that there aren't people out there who can't wait to experience it.

Think outside of the box when it comes to your experience. Think about how your ideal clients want to feel, experience, see, and hear when it comes to buying. Create a sales and buying experience that is perfectly aligned with what they need, how they like to buy and perhaps that added experience on top.

Action points:

Explore and think about your ideal client. How are they likely to like to buy?

What experience do they most like to have?

How can you keep them engaged during the buying process?

Chapter Eight

YOU NEED MORE SPEED

*E*veryone talks about dealing with objections, making sure you deal with objections, being ready to deal with objections, etc. and yet one of the biggest causes of objections happening in the first place isn't necessarily talked about. Most people seem to talk about doing the very opposite of what I'm about to speak about and it surprises me.

Humans by nature are people that want things, like, yesterday. Many people would also say that by nature humans are pretty lazy. I'm not saying I agree with that, but if we think about how our buying habits and processes have changed through the years and how society has changed then actually there's evidence to back it up.

We've gone from having to use cheques and cash to pay for goods to being able to tap watches, phones and having everything available to us at the click of a button. One of the great things about living on an island is that I've saved an absolute fortune not falling victim to that bloody Amazon one click button! I used to have boxes turn up at my door that I had forgotten all about ordering. Some of them never even left their boxes as it was essentially rubbish that I didn't even need.

But it was quick. It was easy. I saw something and one click later it was at my door the next day.

People will spend more these days than before. People will buy things these days with less thought than before. Why? Because your thinking time is less and when it comes to paying in shops you don't feel the same connection to the money that you may once have felt.

Statistically you are more likely to really contemplate whether you need what you're about to buy if you're paying with cash versus paying with your card, watch or online.

Why? Because you are going to be physically handing over cash, in the same way that you are way more likely to really contemplate whether you need what you're about to buy if you're standing in a long queue at a store versus on the computer or when there's no queue.

Why? Because it gives you more thinking time, and in that thinking time your brain has the chance to talk you out of it, to question whether you really need or want it.

Now you might be wondering what any of this has to do with you. You might not sell in stores so you might think this is all a little pointless - but it isn't. This is something that you need to be aware of.

Whilst in the online space you may not have physical queues to purchase from you, there are other barriers you can potentially be putting in people's way. There are queues of sorts that you may well have created and this often causes issues for people.

Why would you want to slow the whole process down? Does it benefit you? Not in the long run and it can make your sales feel a lot harder than they actually are. By slowing the whole process down or putting walls in people's way, you may unknowingly be damaging your conversion rate. People may be pulling out because they have that time to really think, to talk themselves out of saying yes or you might find that something else happens.

People might decide not to even bother, so you lose sales. They may go through the process but by the time it gets to the actual sale they now have a ton of objections and have disconnected with the energy and emotion they felt when they first started the process. This can result in you feeling as if making the sale is hard.

This is really important when it comes to high-ticket selling. Emotion is one of the biggest reasons people buy. If your sales process is too long, has too many walls and you haven't taken into consideration keeping them connected to the emotion of what they want to buy, then you simply don't see the conversions you really desire, meet way more objections and ultimately selling can feel hard.

Which is the total opposite of what you actually desire, right?

We already know you want to be making high-ticket sales with ease because if you didn't you wouldn't be reading this book. Besides, who actually wants to be making sales that feel really difficult or not making enough sales?

If you desire to sell high-ticket or any level with ease then you have to understand the concept of speeding things up versus slowing them down. If you are slowing the process down it's really important to keep people connected in with the emotions of why they want to buy as they're going through the process.

Speed is important. Fewer walls are important. Fewer obstacles are crucial.

I don't know about you but I don't want to have to complete a maze quest in order to be able to buy something. I am the type of person that if there is a long queue in a shop I will put everything back and buy it online! I know I'm a total nightmare but I cannot stand wasting time. Hanging around in a queue is my idea of hell. I could be doing something else with that time and I am way more likely to question whether I even need or want half this stuff whilst I'm in that long queue. By the time I have bought it I've totally lost the excitement or emotion I felt when I first decided to buy it.

Ultimately it ruins the whole experience for me, so why would I actively choose to do that? Why would you actively choose to put your own potential clients through that experience?

But you can't just not have an application form...

I know you're probably thinking of your sales process and thinking about all of the things you couldn't possibly get rid of. You have to have those application forms for example, especially for high-ticket.

Do you, though? What's the actual purpose of the application form for you?

For some of my programmes I have an application form but for most I don't. You could decide to purchase my 200k programme without completing an application form. Why? Because I don't need one.

To begin with, my sales process for that specific programme means I've already spoken to them in some way, shape or form before they're buying. Adding in an application form would therefore do nothing more than lengthen the process out.

I also don't have application forms for various other programmes where my sales process isn't set up to speak to them first. In some cases they can go to my website, find the programme that's perfect for them, click buy, sign the contract and within ten minutes they are paid up, signed up and have received all of their initial welcome pack.

Why would I need the application form? I know my ideal clients like to buy quickly. I know a form would just act as a barrier for them and a barrier with no purpose.

A lot of people use the application form as a way of filtering people out, but I filter people out long before they apply for anything. My positioning, my messaging, my copy, my content and my pricing all filter them out. It is all designed and set up to filter them out.

When I do use an application form it's because the specifics of the programme mean that I have to be 100% sure the individual is a total match and in the exact position I need them to be in, in order to take part. But the application form isn't set up in a way that slows the whole process down.

They don't have to wait for me or someone on my team to look at the application form, they don't have to wait to be emailed any more links, they don't have to wait a further few days to then receive anything else and we don't have to worry about anyone not receiving something or it ending up in their junk.

They fill in the application form, and we use a system that is set up to take their answers and immediately run it through the checker to determine whether they fit the criteria. If they do, they get an immediate next step link on that form completion page which enables them to take the next step in purchasing straight away.

In this case the application form doesn't slow the process down at all because we're using systems behind it that enable us to maintain the speed. The application form serves a purpose but also isn't built in a way that acts like this huge wall people then have to potentially wait days to be able to go any further with.

The question of whether you absolutely need to use application forms is a simple one to answer - the answer is simply no. You don't need to use application forms. You can definitely sell high-ticket without them. Over 90% of my high-ticket sales are done without a single use of an application form and 99.9% of people that become clients are a completely perfect fit.

But if you are going to use application forms then that shouldn't mean the whole process is slowed down or lengthened out. It isn't about having the application form as some sort of wall that slows the whole thing down or gives them an opportunity to then start talking themselves out of what it is they're about to buy.

It's about using the application form for whatever you need it to do for you whilst also finding a way to ensure the process still stays as short, quick and effective as possible. You could use systems; you could make sure all application forms are checked within a couple of hours; you could have clear instructions on the thank you page for what happens next so that no one is left wondering or waiting around.

If you're going to use application forms then be really clear as to why you're using them. What purpose do they serve for you? Is an application form the only way you can serve that purpose? If so how can you ensure the application form doesn't slow things down?

But you can't make a high-ticket sale without speaking to them first!

Why? Who says? I'm saying you don't!

Sometimes the very first time I actually speak to a new high-ticket client is on our first call. Yes, you read that right, sometimes I don't ever speak to them in advance. But when I first came into the online coaching/strategist space, I thought I had to.

Every single person I spoke to seemed to say that you had to do sales calls, you had to do calls before people could buy from you. I was a little perplexed as to why, but thought, "Hey, who am I to argue? If everyone else is doing it then maybe I just need to as well."

And so I did, until I woke myself up! I've never followed rules set by others before. Why did I start now? Just because it's what everyone else was doing, didn't mean it had to be what I did, did it?

I started to play around with the concept of prospective clients not having to talk to me on a call as a standard step everyone had to take. If they wanted to then they could, but it wasn't something they had to do in order to buy from me.

There were some of my online entrepreneur friends who thought I was crazy.

"What if you end up working with people who are the wrong fit?"

"What if people are put off by the price and then you miss out because they won't have spoken to you?"

"What if…"

But for each what if, I had a logical answer and the risk made sense to me.

I knew that the people who were the perfect fit for me were people that liked to just take action and be able to buy quickly. They already knew what they wanted, they already knew if it was a yes and quite frankly, they saw the calls being as tiresome as I did.

It stood to reason that not offering calls as a default would actually further filter the wrong people out, ensuring that I was only attracting my perfect fit into working with me. No one who wasn't the right fit for me would make it all the way through my content, my marketing, my lead system, my sales process and still click buy.

And even if it did, the chances of it happening were so slim it still made sense, because the way the sales process was originally set up meant I was attracting more people who weren't a fit for me onto the call than people that were. When I crunched the numbers I figured that I could drastically increase my conversion rate by making this change.

So I did. I took the "you have to speak to me first" aspect away from all of my offerings at the time, and what happened?

Exactly what I had predicted. I doubled my sales within thirty days having changed nothing other than the sales process. I attracted people who were the absolute perfect fit to work with me and for those who did still reach out and ask for a call, they all converted leaving me with a conversion rate of 100% from any calls that I actually did.

I had saved myself time. I had saved my potential clients time. I had fine-tuned attracting in only those who were a perfect fit to work with me. I had increased my own sales. I had made the process feel a whole lot easier.

Do you absolutely need to speak to them before they can buy?

No, you don't absolutely need to but whether you choose to or not comes down to a few things. Just like the application form, it's understanding what the purpose of the call is and whether a call is actually the only way you can speak to people.

These days I'd argue not. Most people speak to me via email, Facebook, Instagram, LinkedIn and never ask for a call. Conversations can happen in so many different spaces, spaces that mean it can slot into their day rather than having to take a chunk of time out of it. You might also be surprised at how many people point blank try and avoid having to go onto tons of calls.

There are actually plenty of people who get really nervous about going onto calls at all and they'd feel much happier and more comfortable speaking via another platform first, deciding to purchase from there and then obviously having calls if that is part of what they buy from you.

Realistically, for many people offering calls they don't actually serve any real purpose other than to slow things down and potentially even put people off, whilst also not seeing optimum conversions from their sales calls in the process either.

Having people on calls before they buy isn't compulsory for high-ticket. I sell everything from 10k to over 200k and not everyone gets on a call. In fact, the vast majority do not and yet they still buy.

Whether that's right for you is another matter. It depends on your ideal clients and on what the purpose of the call is, but if speaking to them *is* important then just like the application form ensure it doesn't lengthen the process out and cause walls when there really don't need to be.

Simplify the process. Speed it up. Have things sent to them in the meantime before you get to talk to them.

But if you've just got those calls there to satisfy your own fear about not attracting the right people, then maybe it's time you checked on how you're filtering people out because you shouldn't be getting on calls with people who are the wrong fit!

Emotion is one of the biggest driving factors when selling effortlessly

Emotion, it's a big one.

Excitement.

Happiness.

Possibilities.

Dreams.

Fears.

Sadness.

Anger.

Envy.

Emotions play a large part in our lives and they play a large part in selling too. Before I go too far into talking about this in this chapter, I just want to say that I'm going to be covering this from various angles in different chapters as we move forward, but I'm never going to be talking about using negative emotions as a way to scare people into buying. If that's your style then good for you, but it's not mine and I don't recommend it.

You don't need to scare someone into saying yes with you. I much prefer connecting them in with the other emotions. It doesn't just make for a lighter experience but also sets the perfect platform to hit the ground running in a positive way once they're working with me.

But more on that later. For now I want to cover why continuing to connect them into emotions whilst going through your sales process is important. It's important because emotion is one of the biggest driving factors as to why people buy.

It stands to reason that if your sales process is too long, has too many walls or doesn't continue to connect them into those emotions whilst they're waiting to be able to buy from you, what happens is that they're more likely to say no. It's more likely to feel hard and they're more likely to talk themselves out of saying yes.

Can you ever think of an occasion when you've gone from being fired up and excited to feeling the complete opposite a few days or a week later and you've not actually gone ahead? Most of us can, and in some of those cases the reason why that happened is because we didn't stay connected to that excited emotion. Our fears crept in, our doubts crept in, we started to talk ourselves out of it, and we questioned whether we really needed or wanted it. In the end we disconnected with that emotion so much that we just didn't feel the same buzz, and we ended up not going ahead with it.

That's definitely happened for me on more than one occasion and perhaps the same for you. This is why it's so crucially important to really think about your sales process and ensure that you are still connecting them in with those emotions.

This is particularly important if your sales process is slightly longer. Above I mentioned how some of my clients send things to their potential clients as part of the sales process and some of my clients leverage that same approach to keep their potential clients connected in emotionally with what it is they're trying or wanting to buy.

Some of my clients do have longer sales processes often because it involves proposals to be deliberated on, corporate decisions to be made and so on. They've sped the process up as much as they can but to ensure that emotion is still maintained they bring actions into the sales process that keeps the potential clients connected whilst the waiting is happening.

Have you ever ended up on a sales call with someone that a week or so before seemed like they absolutely couldn't wait to say yes, only by the time the call comes around it seems the total opposite? That's also likely because the disconnect from the emotion they were initially feeling has happened - the voices of doubt and fear have crept in. This is also where you find getting the sale can feel like pulling teeth. You're having to constantly convince them, deal with a thousand objections, convince them some more... it's frustrating and extremely draining right?

It can also make you feel as if you just don't enjoy sales at all; sales may be the hardest thing you have come across. Keeping them connected emotionally in this case is going to be like a magic wand for you: it's that emotion that will help you make sales easier, it's that emotion that will reduce the number of objections, and it's that emotion that can help you feel as if you're no longer convincing anyone.

This is of course why it's crucial to get your sales process to be as efficient as possible, to limit the amount of time that people have to disconnect from those emotions. But if you've shortened that process, if you've sped it up as best as you can, if you've perfected it and made it as simple as possible whilst still containing everything your potential clients need, then it's time to think about what you could do to encourage your potential clients to stay emotionally connected.

This could be something extremely simple as having them talk to a current or past client of yours or it could be something a little bigger where they get sent something physical. This of course all depends on who it is you're selling to and it may not even be something you have to worry about too much because your sales process might be extremely quick. It could be that there are no walls and they can go from being interested to buying in a thirty minute window, but if that's not the case then pay attention to the emotions because it's really important if you want to make high-ticket selling feel effortless.

So many people create their sales process acting from the space of fear: fear that pricing will put people off; fear that not speaking to someone will mean they end up working with people they don't like. Fear isn't what you should be thinking of when creating your

buying processes. **You should create them based on speed, efficiency and how your ideal clients actually like to buy.**

Action points:

Think about the points below and then think about how your own sales process should look.

How do your ideal clients like to buy?

What buying experiences have you had that you've enjoyed?

Typically speaking, what do your ideal clients not enjoy having to do in order to be able to buy something?

What do they need to see, hear or experience in order to be ready to buy?

How can you filter the wrong people out without slowing the process down?

Then brainstorm some ways that you can keep them connected during the buying process (if applicable, obviously).

Chapter Nine

THIS MATTERS THE MOST

"People just come to me. I don't chase anyone."

I'm sure you've come across that at some point. If you spend any length of time in the online world I can almost guarantee you will have.

But I have an issue with it. People take it way too literally which then means you have swathes of people sitting there never mentioning that anyone can buy from them and never asking for the sale. They also often haven't thought about what happens behind the scenes in order to have that system where people seem to just flock to someone.

This of course results in people just waiting for someone to reach out and want to work with them, which for most people doesn't ever happen. The whole 'people coming to people' and having that 'in demand' type of feeling isn't an accident. It doesn't just magically happen and it doesn't happen because they never sell either.

It looks effortless to others and it feels effortless to them, but it's not down to luck, it's not down to hoping, and it's not down to hiding what they're selling. It's down to the fact they've taken the right steps and set things up in the right way.

These people didn't wake up one day after putting out tons of free content for seven months and suddenly be seen as 'in demand'. They didn't suddenly have people just radiating towards them and wanting to work with them.

Sales, so effortless it's as easy as breathing.

None of it is an accident. It certainly didn't happen overnight and it's not that they've left it up to luck. But there is a difference between that feeling of having to convince anyone to buy from you versus seemingly have people queuing up to buy from you.

There's a difference between people reaching out and saying, "I want what you're selling," or even just buying it without speaking to you, and you chasing people down every five minutes after they liked your post asking if they want to buy, then following up with them every day after they show an interest to see if they're ready to buy yet.

It's not that you shouldn't follow up. It's not that following up isn't a thing, but there's a difference between following up with a genuine hot lead who just needs a bit of time to get over the line, versus following up with every person who shows the slightest bit of interest in what you do. They could be a week or six months away from being ready to work with you.

The difference comes down to what you do before you get to the sales conversation. The difference is how you're showing up, how you're letting people know they can buy from you and how you're positioning yourself. It's those elements which help someone go from unknown to someone who seems to radiate sales left, right and centre.

It's those elements which help you go from feeling as if you have to convince people to buy from you, pulling teeth and chasing down every sale to effortlessly making sales at every single level, celebrating 10k, 50k, 100k or even higher days with ease.

It is not an accident and none of it is left to luck.

In this case it's actually not about you!

We've spoken a lot in this book about how it is about you, and for large parts of it, it certainly is, but this part actually isn't. Oddly enough, whilst people make it not about them in so many other areas of their business, when it comes to this part they do get wrapped up in themselves.

The issue of positioning really isn't about you. The biggest issue in the aspect of positioning is thinking that it *is* about you.

It happens because you see things differently. In many cases you already know everything that your ideal clients need... of course you do, you are after all the expert in your field. This is brilliant but thinking about it from the expert point of view is certainly not brilliant when it comes to the positioning of what you're selling.

If there was just one thing I could share with someone and tell them, "If you changed this one thing you'd see a big difference in how easy it is to make sales," it would be this.

Positioning.

I'm going to say this repeatedly because it's highly important.

Positioning is KEY.

Positioning is KEY.

Positioning is KEY.

I've had clients who have struggled with selling an offer for months and months, then they change this one thing - change their positioning of the offer - and go from no sales to selling six and even seven figures worth of that offer in the subsequent months.

Because... positioning is key. It is one of the most important factors when it comes to how easy a sale is to make and whether you have people banging down your door to buy it or not.

The issue is that when most people think about the positioning of their offer, they approach it from their point of view, thinking about themselves.

What they think people need.

What they think people want.

But nine times out of ten, that's actually not what people are thinking.

I know why most people aren't making sales without taking a second look at what they're doing. Most people make the same common mistakes BUT if I tried selling them the solution that I actually know they need, and I positioned from that space, I wouldn't make the sales.

What I know they need and what they know they want (and sometimes what they think they need) are often two different things.

When you're trying to sell someone something that you know they need but that they don't, it ends up feeling as if you're having to convince these people that they need what you have. Now, you could continue to do that if you want to. It may be a longer process and it may feel way harder but it's not impossible to make sales like that. It's just not my favoured approach because if you haven't figured it out by now, I don't like to do the whole "sales feeling like really hard work" approach.

Sales should light you up... period. Because they're amazing. FACT!

So why create environments where sales feel anything less than that? Why create environments where sales and selling feels like the opposite of that, where it feels hard, dark and not nice at all? We want sales to feel freeing, exciting, thrilling, joyful, easy... all the things sales and selling deserves to feel like.

And this is why you should be...

"Selling the want and then giving them what they need"

What do I actually mean by that, though?

Forget about how you see something and think about how they see it. Think about what it is that they want right now. That may well be different from what it is you know they actually need.

For example: They want to lose fifty pounds but you know it's actually a change of mindset that they need in order to lose the fifty pounds.

If you try and sell them the change of mindset and you position what you're selling from that perspective, making it about the thing rather than the want/destination, then you'll find yourself convincing people they need what you're selling.

If, however, you position and sell the want, in this case to lose fifty pounds, and then you give them what they need (the mindset changes) it's the same concept as selling the destination versus the aeroplane itself.

It's not about positioning selling the coaching, the service, the thing itself, it's positioning yourself from the point of selling the want and destination. The positioning should be focused on the want, on the destination and not on the thing itself.

This is where you have to forget about yourself for a second. This is where you have to think about what your ideal clients want and how they see things. Trying to sell them something that they don't know they need doesn't work; trying to sell them something that they don't know they want doesn't work.

It can work if you're ready to spend ages convincing them that they need it, but I know that's not how you want to feel about the sales that you make and so it stands to reason that you don't want to be positioning yourself in that way.

Do you think people are flocking to buy from others because they're selling something that the people they're selling to don't know they need or want? No. They're flocking to them, they're reaching out to them, they're queuing up to buy from them because they've positioned what they sell perfectly to hit the want and destination of the people they're selling to.

You'll always see things differently because you are an expert at what you do and sell. You do it day in and day out. You're IN IT so you see things differently. You can already do what they can't; you can already see what they can't; what they find difficult, you find easy. That's why they're going to be buying from you, no matter what it is that you're selling.

But when it comes to your positioning, you're going to have to detach from that. You need to understand exactly what your ideal clients want from their point of view, what destination they desire from their point of view and you can then use that to create positioning that means you can sell your offer with ease and no longer feel as if you're convincing people to work with you.

Your own positioning also matters!

In the same way that the positioning of what you sell matters, so does your own positioning. There are two sides to this and I'm going to cover both right here. The first part is thinking that if you want to be seen as someone who people flock to buy from then being a jack of all trades is not going to be a good look for you. That creates the opposite effect to the one that you likely want to create. Why would people flock to someone who works with everyone and does everything?

This is where your own positioning comes in. The more in demand or the more you have an element of a buzz around you, the more likely it is people are going to queue up to work with you. It's simply one of those things.

This won't happen, however, or will at least be much harder to achieve, if you blend into the background with everyone else in your field. If you're not positioning yourself in a way that helps you stand out, you're going to have a tough time creating that buzz or 'in demand' aspect of things.

The first thing to think of here is how to separate yourself out from all of the noise. This is highly important when it comes to high-ticket selling. To sell high-ticket with ease you do have to be seen as being "high-ticket worthy" so to speak.

This isn't about fancy websites, massive numbers, polished images or any of that. It's actually much simpler than any of that. It's about positioning yourself as being specialised in a field, being an expert in an area or spending your time working with a specialised area.

Why does this make a difference?

When you do this, you're instantly seen differently. Instantly you raise yourself above all of the noise that's out there and you get seen. It also helps from a high-ticket perspective. They'll see an offer which is specialised towards the want and destination they desire and then it's being carried out by someone who specialises in working with them.

It's like an instant megaphone that gets you heard by the right people, cuts through the noise and elevates your positioning.

You can do this no matter what field you're in. Even if you're a graphic designer you can specialise your services towards a specific niche, providing specialised destinations and wants for them. If you want to be heard above the noise and elevate your positioning, this is going to be key!

The other factor is how you're seen and how people feel when they see you. Let's say for example you want to give off the exclusive feeling... one of exclusivity, luxury, richness. That's amazing, but if you're then giving off the energy and image of being the opposite of that, what do you think happens?

Imagine you're saying that you're exclusive and yet in the next breath you're running a mass free challenge for everyone and their dog to join. There'll be a disconnect, right?

Contrary to what you might think, you don't have to be front and centre with thousands upon thousands of raving fans to achieve the sales you desire. Now it may be that's exactly what you want and if it is, that's amazing, but if it's not then you definitely do not have to go down that route.

I have clients who you'll never see running free challenges. Some of them don't even use social media and yet they sell out all of their offers. They operate in an extremely private, exclusive way and that works for them, the vision they have, what they feel aligned with and the people they actually want to be working with.

In the same way, there'd be a disconnect if you wanted to create this big buzzy energy around yourself and yet no one saw you anywhere and had no chance to ever connect with you. There'd be a disconnect between what you wanted and the vibe you were creating.

Why is this important?

It's important because if you're going to effortlessly attract in the people you want to be working with and make those sales, then the vibe you give off in your own positioning has to match what will align with what they desire, what they're looking for and also the vibe you want to create.

It's like Ferrari saying that they're luxury and yet everyone and their dog is driving around in one of their cars after buying them for a ridiculously low price.

I know online it can be difficult. If you want to reach your success and make the sales you desire, you may think that your only option is to do what those ones you see everywhere are doing. You might think that even though you don't want to and even though deep down you know that's not what your ideal clients would be looking for, you have no option but to be everywhere, sell at every level, have free challenges left, right and centre. That's not the case.

Remember the ones that you see everywhere are doing the model that's right for them and who they're looking to work with; their positioning is right for them. You see them because that's the whole point, but that doesn't mean there aren't people out there doing what you desire to do, positioning themselves in the way you desire, taking action in the way you desire that may not involve being seen by the masses and still they're killing it. You just haven't seen them because that's kind of the whole point. You might not be their ideal client and so would never need to be on their radar and see them.

What's important to know here is that you might find that there are different layers to your business and the different layers mean you can show up and have slightly different positioning for each one.

What's also important to remember is that I'm not saying that you have to be this big secret. In fact for many of you it probably isn't what you desire and that's absolutely fine. I mean, I sell high-ticket but I have no desire to be a big secret.

What is important is that you understand what you do want, what your ideal clients would be looking for and what vibe you want to give off with your positioning. If you're not clear, it's going to be a mess and you could potentially take yourself down a path that you do not want to go down.

Your positioning matters. It plays a crucial role in whether you have that element of people radiating towards you and people buying from you effortlessly. This largely hangs on you getting your positioning right!

A client once told me how they only ever seemed to attract the very opposite of the person they wanted to be working with and they couldn't figure out why. The why was easy: their positioning was totally off. Not only had they positioned what they were selling in the wrong way but they'd also positioned themselves in the wrong way, on the one hand wanting one type of client but on the other positioning themselves and showing up for another.

There was a total disconnect between what they wanted and what they were actually saying they were available for and were for.

Don't be disconnected when it comes to your positioning. Be clear and stick with it!

There's also something a little deeper to think about with your positioning

When it comes to positioning yourself for effortless selling you may also want to keep this in mind. Earlier in the book I talked about how people like to buy in different ways, some people are driven highly by emotion and want to buy quickly, others take a little more time and are less emotionally driven, more practical as such, but there's also another angle to consider that's specific to high ticket and it fits into what you may want to take into consideration when it comes to your positioning and that is…....

Why do people buy high ticket?! (or luxury as a whole)

They buy just because you have something they want, right? Well yes and no, there are other aspects that come into play when they choose to buy high ticket, let's be clear not everyone does buy high ticket, in fact many people will go through their whole lives never buying anything high ticket or luxury in any way shape or form. But people who pay high ticket will generally do so for these 3 reasons:

There's also something a little deeper to think about with your positioning

When it comes to positioning yourself for effortless selling you may also want to keep this in mind. Earlier in the book I talked about how people like to buy in different ways, some people are driven highly by emotion and want to buy quickly, others take a little more time and are less emotionally driven, more practical as such, but there's also another angle to consider that's specific to high ticket and it fits into what you may want to take into consideration when it comes to your positioning and that is…...

Why do people buy high ticket?! (or luxury as a whole)

They buy just because you have something they want, right? Well yes and no, there are other aspects that come into play when they choose to buy high ticket, let's be clear not everyone does buy high ticket, in fact many people will go through their whole lives never buying anything high ticket or luxury in any way shape or form. But people who pay high ticket will generally do so for these 3 reasons:

1. They want to work with and buy what they deem is the best
2. They buy to fulfill a bit of an ego trip and/or buy for the connections that could potentially be made as a result of buying from that person and/or they buy because of the person that is

delivering the service (an example..work with someone who they think is well connected or a big name as such)

3. They're looking for speed, an experience or a container that appeals to the way they desire to work.

Why does this matter? Because it can play into the actions you take to position yourself in the way that will get your ideal clients flocking to buy from you and it can also help you determine what areas to pay attention to when it comes to your marketing.

Now it could be a case that your ideal clients buy high ticket because of a combination of the above and you can then bring a little bit of all of it into your own positioning and focus. But if you know that your ideal clients are more likely to buy because of the experience then you'd ensure that was a focus of your marketing, you'd also make sure that you had positioning that really centered around the amazing experience working with you or buying from you provides.

In the same way that if it's because they deem someone to be the best then you would need to think about what qualifies someone as being the best in their eyes and how you can achieve that level of positioning yourself.

If you think about it this can also help you when

deciding on how to deliver your services, if you know that your ideal clients are likely paying high ticket for speed then you'd want to be creating services that delivered that outcome.

A fun exercise with this is for you to take a look at why you've purchased a high ticket offer or service (if you have) . If not , you can think about the high ticket purchase you do desire to purchase. What attracts you? Why is that a high ticket that you desire to have or did buy?

You'll likely find your reasons either fit into a combination of the above or just one. Pay attention to this when thinking about your positioning, there has to be a reason why your ideal clients desire to buy a high ticket offer and whilst the result they're going to get does of course feature in that there is also wider reasonings that also play out.

Why does this matter? Because it can play into the actions you take to position yourself in the way that will get your ideal clients flocking to buy from you and it can also help you determine what areas to pay attention to when it comes to your marketing.

Now it could be a case that your ideal clients buy high ticket because of a combination of the above and you can then bring a little bit of all of it into your own positioning and focus. But if you know that your ideal clients are more likely to buy because of the experience then you'd ensure that was a focus of your marketing, you'd also make sure that you had positioning that really centered around the amazing experience working with you or buying from you provides.

In the same way that if it's because they deem someone to be the best then you would need to think about what qualifies someone as being the best in their eyes and how you can achieve that level of positioning yourself.

If you think about it this can also help you when deciding on how to deliver your services, if you know that your ideal clients are likely paying high ticket for speed then you'd want to be creating services that delivered that outcome.

A fun exercise with this is for you to take a look at why you've purchased a high ticket offer or service (if you have) . If not , you can think about the high ticket purchase you do desire to purchase. What attracts you? Why is that a high ticket that you desire to have or did buy?

You'll likely find your reasons either fit into a combination of the above or just one. Pay attention to this when thinking about your positioning, there has to be a reason why your ideal clients desire to buy a high ticket offer and whilst the result they're going to get does of course feature in that there is also wider reasonings that also play out.

Don't forget to have others help you

When it comes to positioning yourself in a way that makes sales effortless you can't look far past having others help spread the word about you and your work. That could be through collaboration, referrals or having people feature you.

Others sharing you with their network and audience is really important if you want to make sales effortlessly whilst also not having to do all of the marketing yourself either.

The world aren't mind readers

Let's clear something up. Contrary to what it may sound like, having the feeling of people banging down your door, and effortlessly selling what you do, does not come down to you never mentioning that you have something for sale.

It just doesn't. Sure it may happen occasionally that someone will randomly ask how they could buy from you, but the vast majority of the time that isn't how it works. If you don't let people know they can buy from you, exactly why would they even be banging down your door anyway? How does not letting people know they can buy from you and work with you help you when it comes to selling and making effortless sales? When you think about it logically you're actually making it harder!

It's harder because they're having to guess if they can buy anything from you. Whilst some people will reach out and ask anyway, there's a larger percentage who won't. They're far more likely to assume you don't sell anything or there's no way to really work with you.

You're doing the opposite of many things I've talked about in this book: the speeding the process up, the not having roadblocks and walls in people's way to buy.

Those are all crucial aspects when it comes to effortlessly selling. By not actually letting people know they can ever buy anything, you slow the whole process down. You put one giant massive wall in their way by saying they have to actually ask you whether they can even buy anything in the first place. They are far more likely to go elsewhere, to the person who is openly saying that you can work with them.

There is one little point I want to make... depending on who you're selling to, this doesn't necessarily mean that you plaster your social media every day letting people know they can buy from you. Remember we've already talked about people buying in different ways and the fact is that your ideal clients may not even be on social media buying. How you let them know they can buy from you might look very different.

It could require some out of the box thinking, but either way you'd still in some way, shape or form be letting them know they can buy from you. It doesn't matter where that happens, just that it does happen. It doesn't really matter "where" - just that you do.

I mean, why wouldn't you want to let people know?

I know for a lot of people there's the element of being worried people would judge them for selling, or that they'd look salesy or pushy. We've already covered why that isn't the case anyway, but I often think that if that's why people don't actually ask for the sale as such, then the logic behind it is a little flawed.

If you're saying that you don't mention people can buy from you because you're worried about being seen as salesy, or judged for even charging for what you do, then how does not asking for the sale change that in a way that means people would then reach out and ask to buy from you?

If someone is going to judge you for selling then I can almost guarantee they're not an ideal client of yours and would in all likelihood not actually buy from you anyway. If someone is going to disagree with you charging for what you do then how does not asking for the sale change that? They're not ever going to pay to work with you anyway. They disagree with it so why would they?

And yet you're making a decision to act and essentially to try and please people who would never have bought from you in the first place.

But what about all those other people that actually do want to pay you? The ones that value what you do? The ones that want what you do?

They don't get the opportunity or chance because you're acting from trying to please the people who aren't your people. The logic is a little flawed when you think about it, right?

I know there are plenty of people out there who think I shouldn't charge for what I do or charge as much as I do, but here's the thing to keep in mind. I've honed my skills and knowledge over a decade and more. When working with me you get access to my brain (I think and see things differently, which in most cases is priceless) but equally you get to make amazing returns from my knowledge. If someone is going to profit 10k, 100k, 1million, 10million and more from my help, why wouldn't I be getting a small percentage of that?

Those people who think that are simply not my people and I don't desire to have them in my world. I'm not going to let them stop me from serving the people who are my people.

In the end all you're really doing is making it difficult for the people who are your people, who need what it is that you do and who can't wait to buy your service. You don't want to make it difficult for them, so stop focusing on the people who don't matter!

Action points:

What is the destination or want that my ideal clients have that I can use in my positioning?

What can I specialise in to help elevate my positioning?

What's important for me to think of when it comes to the vibe of my positioning?

Who are the types of people I should be collaborating with or appearing with to help raise my positioning?

How can I remember to ask for the sale and make it as easy as possible for people to know they can buy from me?

En objection doesn't mean

Chapter Ten

IT'S NOT A NO

*A*n objection doesn't mean that they're not an ideal client of yours!

I often see this said online and I even have people ask me about it. For some people it may well be a case that they have a boundary that says if someone has an objection, they're not buying from me, and that's fine. I don't quite understand it, but each to their own. However, it's not how I see it. Objections are normal but sometimes we just don't see them or come across them as often because our processes and strategies might be set up to eliminate them before they come to the surface (I'll talk more about this further on in this chapter).

But why is someone having an objection a bad thing? It isn't. I mean, it's completely natural; people have objections all the time, even when they don't really see it as an objection as such.

An objection certainly doesn't mean they aren't willing to buy from you, or pay you, it just means they have a question. Sometimes those questions are bigger than others; sometimes they hold someone back more than others might be held back.

There are five core areas where people usually have objections:

Budget

Trust

Need

Urgency

Time

Generally speaking they're fairly valid objections. It's not unreasonable to have an objection when you don't have a big enough budget; it's not unreasonable to have an objection when they may not know you yet.

But objections can be overcome; in fact they regularly are. Just because someone has an objection doesn't mean they don't buy. They could also have objections at any stage of the process with you. Some people even have objections crop up for them before they even comment on a post on Facebook.

Objections to taking action aren't limited to just sales. People can have objections to taking any sort of action: signing up to an email list, commenting on Facebook… you would be amazed if you knew how many people have to talk themselves INTO commenting on a Facebook post!

It sounds crazy and yet it happens, but for the most part people work through their objections and you may never know they had any. You might even be working through objections with people and not even realise you're doing it.

That is, until it comes to selling, where when someone receives an objection they often freeze and panic…

"OMG, how will I respond without sounding pushy?"

"They clearly don't want it then."

The number of sales that are not converted because an objection rears its head is insane. What's crazy is that the person who made the objection often goes and buys elsewhere which shows that had the objection just been handled they would have bought!

An objection does not mean that it's a no. It doesn't mean that person won't buy. It just means they have an objection.

And you trying to alleviate those objections or talk through the objections with them is not a pushy sales tactic or approach, although I get why it feels like that. It's because you start to overthink things and create this massive story in your head. You overthink by questioning every word you're thinking of saying... "Is that too much? Is that too pushy? Will that sound wrong?"

Before you know it you also have this huge story in your head how they'll think you're pushy, desperate for sales or anything else if you dared to approach the objection or talk about it. Let's be logical here - that's crazy.

Not only is it crazy because the chances of it happening are slim to none, but also because the fact you're even worrying about it just goes to show that you would never actually be that pushy person you're afraid of being. As long as you were coming from a place of alignment yourself, tapping into your own sales power, remembering that it's just a conversation, you'd never be pushy. It would be the total opposite to who you are anyway!

Objections are opportunities to explore further with your ideal clients. You can actually find a ton of stuff out when exploring conversions that you can use moving forward in other areas. You can even use it to try and deal with objections before they happen.

Be proactive instead of reactive!

Dealing with objections before they reach the point of buying is a great way to not only speed a process up but also help you feel as if you're making sales effortlessly. If we're talking high-ticket sales then being proactive with your objection handling rather than being reactive is definitely something you want to consider.

For most people they don't think about handling objections until the objections smack them in the face, when they're on a call or when they receive the email or message, for example. I actually very rarely receive objections. I can't remember the last sales conversation I had even with my highest ticket clients where I had a ton of objections, not because they didn't have any but because we had already dealt with them long before they got to the point of speaking to me or clicking the buy button.

If we think through the most common objections **(Budget, Trust, Need, Urgency & Time)** they can in some cases be dealt with in other areas of your process, even before people really enter your process.

Budget, for example, can be dealt with on a sales page if you are using one. If you demonstrate value and return, this helps with the budget objection. If you're offering payment plans then again, this helps there.

Trust can be dealt with in your content. You could use trust tags, client results, etc. to help build trust. Even a video where they see you rather than just written content goes a long way in handling the trust objection. You'll build trust quicker with someone if they're off your email list and engaging with you somewhere that they can see and hear you.

Need is an objection that generally can be overcome by positioning towards the want and destination, which then takes away the question of *do I need this?* They know they need this because it's positioned towards the want that they actually have.

Urgency: this objection and how to overcome it largely depends on who it is you're selling to and what you're selling. It could be urgency from the aspect of there being reason for them to say yes now because it'll be available next month anyway. You could overcome this by creating limited spaces and not having the doors constantly open. But it could be urgency from the aspect of it not being something they think they need right now. The way to overcome that, of course, is to position towards what they do want right now or accept that someone who isn't in a place where they need it right now isn't actually your ideal client.

Time as an objection can be overcome by showing them in advance how many hours they may have to dedicate or how much time it would take on their part.

There are so many objections that can be dealt with upfront, but there's one thing that people do, which they think is dealing with objections, that drives me insane...

"I won't sell to you."

If someone does not want to buy from you, does not want to be sold to, literally does not want to buy anything, why on earth are you trying to get them into your sales process or, worse still, on a sales call?

Let's be brutally honest here. Whilst you're saying it's not a sales call, the reason you're getting on the call with them is because you want them to buy from you even if that's not right now. Eventually you do want them to buy.

So it's curious that people use the "I'm not selling anything" as a way to overcome an objection just to get people on calls.

Does it actually work?

Sure, people might get on the call, but are they your ideal clients? Highly unlikely. Are they ready to buy anything? Probably not and worse still, you've just told them you're willing to give away your time and knowledge for free.

Is that the vibe you want to give off?

And it boggles my mind because the people who do this will then be the same ones complaining that everyone is willing to take their free stuff but don't buy anything from them, when that's exactly what they're telling people they do. They're advertising the fact that you can come and take free information and not have to buy anything.

If someone does not want to buy what you're selling, then don't sell to them. When they're ready to buy then sell to them, but telling someone you won't sell to them just as a way to get them to talk to you, only to hope that they will then buy from you is counter-productive and a waste of your time.

In the same way as I don't recommend using "I won't be selling anything" as a way to convince more people to join your free anything, why would you want to fill your audience with people who don't actually want to buy from you?

Quality trumps quantity every time!

Tell people how much time commitment they need to help them overcome their time commitment objection.

Show people the value so they can overcome the value objection.

Share with people your expertise so you can overcome the trust objection.

But don't take yourself down a hole of trying to overcome a sales objection by committing to not even selling anything in the first place! Learn the difference between a genuine objection and someone who's just not your ideal client or not ready to buy from you.

As a side note, as I mentioned earlier, people are a lot wiser than others give them credit for. They're also growing tired and bored of those methods - many will see it and roll their eyes. Even if you put "I'm not selling anything" a lot of people will actually assume that you are. People are wise to those marketing methods, and they're growing tired and bored of a lot of it.

Using those methods could be putting off the very people who would love to buy from you!

I don't want to be pushy.

Of course you don't - who wants to actually be pushy? I mean, let's remember that those pushy cold calls that you have from call centres are only actually pushy because they're on ridiculously tight time lines, commission or have someone breathing down their neck telling them to speed it up because they need more sales!

They don't want to be pushy, and they don't set out to be pushy either, and unfortunately they've been given a script and just told to follow it. They don't understand who they're really speaking to, they're not really told to have a conversation, it's just *read this and sell.*

Now you know that doesn't work and you don't even enjoy being on the other end of it, so why would you ever be like that anyway? In reality you won't, but when you think about dealing with objections when they do come up, people often jump straight to that conclusion.

How do I do this without being pushy?

As if being pushy is a default, as if by exploring or working through an objection with someone you're automatically being pushy, when that isn't the case.

Just imagine how many people you leave hanging because of this thinking. They don't have an objection because they don't want to work with you, they don't have an objection because they don't want to buy from you, they have one because they have a genuine question and perhaps an obstacle.

So let's set the scene. They've gone through your process, they're definitely interested in what you do, they know they want it, they've even imagined themselves saying yes, and then they have a question. They may feel it's a small obstacle and so they mention it to you, and instead of helping them work through it, you just say, "Ok, when you're ready let me know. Bye!"

Here they are, totally left hanging.

They wanted to buy. They just had an objection that they were willing to work through, but you didn't because you didn't want to be pushy.

You don't get the sale. They don't get what they wanted. No one wins.

Handling objections does not mean you need to be pushy. If someone has an objection regarding price it doesn't mean you have to respond with, "Take out a credit card," which is actually one of my pet hates Encouraging people to get into debt is not a good look and does not lend itself to a great sales experience for you or for them. But you could explore other options with them, whether that's payment plans or perhaps a different offer that would be possible for them currently. Dealing with an objection doesn't mean you have to go straight to the extreme. It also doesn't mean that the person will even feel like you're being pushy.

Essentially all you're doing is having a conversation with them, a conversation to explore if there's a way to help them with that objection. Let's not forget that's typically all a sales conversation ever is, a conversation between you and the potential client. A conversation where you're helping them see if it's for them and if they have objections it's just a further conversation to see if those objections can be managed, alleviated or dealt with in some way.

It is not the end of the world if someone has an objection. It doesn't mean they don't want to buy from you. It doesn't mean you have to become that pushy salesperson who will demand they take out credit, sell their house or anything else until you get them to say yes.

And ultimately if, after you have talked through the objection and tried to find solutions, it's still not possible, then that's ok too. You could arrange a follow up. You can arrange to chat again in the future.

They won't think any less of you. They won't feel like they've had a bad experience. They'll feel as if you really listened and tried to help them, which will be of benefit to you moving forward.

The follow up doesn't mean hounding them

Just like the dealing with objections doesn't mean you have to be pushy, dealing with a follow up doesn't mean hounding them every single day until they say yes.

The issue with following up is much like the overcoming objections aspect. People are afraid to do it because of ideas they have around how it will feel or has to look. Often they're overcomplicating the whole process which again results in them just not doing it.

Following up is often seen as something you're doing if you're chasing the sale, while it really isn't. I have a follow up system. Even though I make plenty of sales and have new leads coming in, I'll still follow up.

Following up isn't being desperate, it's actually continuing to be of service. I appreciate people who follow up with me when I'm looking to buy something. I'm a pretty busy person and so sometimes I forget things, sometimes things slip out of my mind, not because I don't want to buy it but because I'm human and life happens.

So when people follow up with me I'm grateful for it. I'm grateful because it's reminded me to take action on something. I'm grateful because I did actually need it. If they didn't follow up nothing would change for me. If they didn't follow up I wouldn't be able to buy whatever it was that I needed.

Now you could say that if I really needed it I wouldn't need reminding... I'm not perfect, I am entirely human (unfortunately I know!) and so whilst I'd love to sit here and say I never ever forget anything and always remember to follow through on everything I need etc., I don't. I'm human and so are the people you're selling to.

99% of the time I'll buy there and then but on the rare occasion I don't it's genuinely because I have needed to check something or perhaps I'm even weighing up a few options. In fact, I recently had that experience.

I was hiring for a new service, and I was trying to choose between a few different options. Out of the five people I spoke to only two followed up with me and I actually ended up hiring them both, one for something slightly different than originally planned. The one that I was originally going to go with didn't follow up with me and so I went elsewhere.

Imagine if you're the one who doesn't do the following up? Imagine if no one followed up with that person who needs what you sell? You could potentially be leaving the very amount you want to increase your sales by on the table just by not following up.

You could potentially double your sales just by following up and with the right system it isn't even any additional work for you, not really. In my first book (She Lives Limitlessly) I talked about how you can follow up and one of the things I talked about was the importance of making someone feel valued when following up.

People think following up is about messaging or ringing regularly to see if they're ready to buy, but it isn't! Following up effectively in a way that still makes the sale feel effortless when it happens and also does it in a way that doesn't feel pushy is to continue the conversation and approach the follow up like an extension of the relationship that has just been started.

One of my clients does this particularly well. As part of their follow up they will have a member of their team search out content or something else that is relevant to the lead they're following up with and then they send it to them. It works amazingly well because it makes that individual feel valued. It makes them feel as if my client is continuing to show interest, pay attention and care about them. It's simple but extremely effective.

You could dial this up on a grander scale and send physical items - there are a million and one ways that you can get creative with it - but the one thing you should not do is think of it as just sending another message or calling again. You have to think about how you can follow up in a way that continues to build the relationship, that makes that individual feel valued.

Think of your follow up process as an extension of that sales process and buying process we spoke about earlier. You want to continue to have them connected in with the emotions that excite them; you want to continue to have them on a journey with you that further connects them into why they should say yes and do this with you.

Sometimes it's about reminding them you're even there and that you valued the fact they took the time to consider buying from you. I have a client who sends a personalised bottle of vintage champagne to every person they have a sales consultation with. I'm not able to share exactly why they do this or the full strategy behind it but I can say that the reason it's done is because they know their ideal clients' buying habits inside out, they know precisely what drives them to say yes to buying from people and they know what their ideal clients value. They have an insane conversion rate from their sales consultations. 97% of every sales consultation they have converts within six months and that is largely down to their amazing sales and buying process with a follow up process that perfectly extends that for anyone who isn't ready to say yes straight away.

Following up doesn't mean that the sale has to become

hard and it doesn't mean you're pushy. Equally, following up isn't something you should only do if you're not making sales and don't have a good flow of leads... following up is just good business sense. They're leads, they're already there, why would you not want to convert them?

Action points:

What are the common objections my ideal clients will have?

How can I proactively deal with them?

How could I follow up in a way that further builds relationships?

Chapter Eleven

MY SECRET SPRINKLES OF MAGIC

*E*ven when I had no proof that I could sell a single thing, I never doubted I'd be successful. I never doubted I'd be rich, I never doubted I'd build successful businesses and I have embodied that belief from the moment I started my first business.

When people ask me what my biggest secret to success and selling is, it's always this part. I could talk about all the strategies under the sun, but the biggest secret to selling successfully, effortlessly and reaching the level of success I desired has and always will be *me* and more importantly the belief I embody.

Which is why it's exactly what I'm going to talk about last before sharing with you my full signature system on selling high-ticket effortlessly.

I never really considered that I was the key and I was the

person who made the most difference to my results. I never considered myself different from others either - I just do me. It all naturally comes to me and makes logical sense. So it was only when I started to work with people that I noticed not everyone approaches it in the same way I do, not everyone thinks like I do or even sees things the way I do.

And it wasn't until much more recently that someone pointed out to me that the thing I think of as being the most normal for me is actually the biggest challenge others have, and so I'm going to share with you a secret system I have that means when I set a sales goal, no matter how large, I hit it. It is the secret system that means I expect to make sales with ease and embody it in every area of my life.

Most people think of selling as being this separate thing, this skill. As we've talked about multiple times in the book, I just don't see it that way, I see it as something that is flowing through every area of our life because it is flowing through us all the time. Selling isn't something we should switch on and switch off - the actual moment we ask for the sale, maybe, but selling as a whole, no.

Your success with a sale starts long before you're actually in a conversation, long before someone is browsing your sales page or you're in the meeting itself. It begins with you, that morning, that week, that month and that year.

We directly see what we believe, we will directly receive what we believe, it is just how it all works even if we're not consciously aware of it.

When I walked into my first board meeting at a large European corporation to deliver a pitch, I had no proof I could do it. I had never done it before but I never once worried that I'd hear no. I never once worried I'd fail. I never once doubted I could do it.

I had prepared. I had prepped as much as I possibly could.

But my preparation wasn't just about conducting research or studying how to pitch effectively, how to deliver presentations or any of that. My preparation began months before and didn't involve anything other than what I'm about to share.

It was about preparing myself. It was about creating the right environment for myself and stepping into a space where it was already a done deal. I have made success and success with sales a done deal for myself for as long as I can remember... doing so totally changed my world and maybe it can change yours too!

A done deal begins inside of you

What do I mean when I say "done deal"? Essentially I mean that you have already decided that whatever it is you're aiming for, trying to achieve or desire is already yours. It's just a case of when it's going to happen and not if it will happen.

It isn't about finding external things to prove to you that it's a done deal and neither is it about waiting until it happens for you to tick it off as a done deal, it's about it being a done deal from the moment you actually decide that it is.

This is something I swear by. Every goal I have ever set, every intention I have ever desired has always happened for me when I come from this space, and when they don't it's because I never made them a done deal to begin with.

I decide. I decide and so it is done!

I decided I was going to move abroad and even decided when it was going to happen long before I knew where. I decided in late 2018 that in the summer of 2019 I was moving abroad. I had no idea where but from that moment I made it a done deal: it wasn't IF I move, it was WHEN I move next summer…

When making plans for the year I referenced the fact that I'd of course be moving in the summer. It was never in doubt. I stepped in and made it a total non-negotiable done deal from the moment I decided it was going to be.

Of course, it's a lot more than just deciding. Along with deciding it's also about stepping into the space where you're embodying the version of you where it is a done deal.

Now let me be really clear - this isn't about you deciding you're a millionaire then going out there telling everyone you are and buying a yacht! That's not what we're talking about here. In fact you can step into the version of you who's already achieving that. You can step into the non-negotiable without having to go and purchase the physical things you would if you were already there.

It wouldn't be about buying the yacht, for example. It would be about understanding the energy of buying the yacht, as in if the version of you who was already there would buy a yacht what feelings would that create for that version of you? It could create a feeling of excitement or fun, for example, so in the now you'd look to bring more of that excitement and fun into your life right now, giving you the same type of energy and feeling you'd have if you were already there, just done in a different way.

Why is all of this important and why do I swear by it? It's simple really. Our actions breed the results we desire. It's from our actions that we see the results we desire and our actions are born from us. They are created from our thoughts, our energy and our ideas. When you are operating from the space in which you are versus the one in which you desire to be, your actions will match where you are versus where you desire to be.

A common question I ask my clients is, "What would you do if you were already where you desired to be?"

The reason I ask that question is because in the answer lies exactly what they're missing and currently not doing. If people were in a position where they expected to make sales with ease and sell high-ticket on repeat, they'd take different actions.

They'd feel more confident to begin with and would likely ask for the sale more. They wouldn't feel as attached to the sale in the first place, enabling it to flow a lot better. They wouldn't go chasing after sales because they would know they don't need to. They'd likely take different actions and show up in some different spaces. They'd potentially pitch and put themselves forward for things they would normally talk themselves out of.

And that's largely the whole idea: to get to where you want to be you'd likely be taking some kind of different action or approach. You'd potentially be a slightly different person and so stepping into that person is crucial when it comes to getting there, in making it happen.

I see people talk about how reaching their goals always feel so hard and yet I sit there and sometimes even forget I was aiming for a goal. Reaching my goals never feels hard because when I am aiming for my goals I am doing so from a place of alignment.

I will have already aligned myself with that goal being a done deal for me. I will have already aligned myself with that on an inner level.

I don't doubt it. I have no reason to. I don't need proof; I've decided it will happen and I will take the action to make it happen. I don't need proof to show me I can, I know that I can!

What does all of this have to do with selling effortlessly?

It has everything to do with it. When you step into a place where it's a done deal, you will take different action, your energy changes and as a result you find your sales change.

The version of you who is effortlessly selling six figures on repeat every single month is different from the version of you right now, whether that's a different mindset, energy, beliefs, actions... they are different and if you want to make it happen and do so whilst feeling like it's effortless, then you want to tap into that version of you now, bring that version into your life now and make it a done deal in the inner game.

Tap into future you energy.

Tap into future you actions.

Tap into future you... it's the key!

It starts before you even get into the action

I'm talking about the sale. The chance of that sale happening is likely decided long before you get into the real action part of it. It doesn't all hinge on whether you say the right thing on the call or that video or presentation. It helps and of course it plays a part, but it's not THE only part that counts.

You start the process for the sale happening before all of that. You decide how easy or hard that sale is going to be hours or potentially days before. I'm not talking about what you think or believe, I'm talking about your own confidence and energy.

We all thrive in different situations with different energies. Just writing this book is proof of that. Some people would be writing this book with noise cancellation headphones and some with candles burning. I'm writing it with Eminem blasting in my headphones. I don't create well in silence but plenty of other people do. Silence is the worst thing for me when it comes to creating. It just doesn't work for me.

But when it comes to my selling energy I don't generally put Eminem on. It's still music but it's a different style of music. Then again, I know people who need to calm themselves down with some quiet before they go into sales conversations, calls or whatever it may be.

I bring a different energy to various areas of my activities. This is a concept I have used since forever when it comes to selling, and more recently I have been introduced to it as something to bring into my schedule as a whole for every activity that I do. It makes total sense and it's actually something I now swear by.

I have a ritual for almost everything that I do and if I haven't been able to batch my activities I'll ensure there's time in between the change of activity to have my bridging time. This is the time that enables me to do whatever I need to do in order to move from one energy into another.

So many people jump into their sales calls, lives, presentations, whatever it may be whilst being in the energy zone that doesn't fuel them in a sales environment. It's like going on stage. Your energy is going to be different on stage than it would be if you were just standing in your living room chatting to some friends or family. If you're trying to sell from an energy that's off, you will feel it. You'll feel yourself totally butting heads with it; it could feel like one of the most frustrating, painful experiences. But when you're in an energy space where you flow, you'll feel differently. When your energy is in alignment, you can flow. When you flow, your sales flow and they flow effortlessly.

Half the challenge with making something feel easier and be easier is creating the environment in which it can be easier. Something is never going to be easier when you're trying to have it perform or exist in an environment that's difficult for it.

We all have optimum performance zones. We may even have different times of the day when we can perform some things better than others. I'm not a morning person. Creating in the morning is not something I can do but at ten at night I am golden. I don't perform best at that time of the day when it comes to selling either. There's little point in my scheduling in a sales activity first thing in the morning.

These are all really simple things but make a huge amount of difference. If you try to have your sales or selling energy flow at a time that is the total opposite to when you actually thrive, it will feel hard.

But I get it - you might not always be in a situation where you can schedule in that activity for when you're at your optimum time. Even though that's something you should be aiming for, it isn't always possible. When it's not possible you need to have routines that help you step into that optimum zone as much as possible.

For me that includes putting on some music and dancing around to increase my energy before I go into the sales activity or environment. For you it may be lighting a candle and standing in front of a mirror, reminding yourself that you make sales effortlessly and people cannot wait to buy from you.

Whilst we're talking energy, that also includes how you feel and what you're thinking. It's ok to be nervous and is totally natural to be nervous. I still get nervous now but those nerves are not the energy that will dominate that activity or situation. It's not my nerves that will dictate my energy. Being nervous is absolutely fine, but being nervous and allowing the nerves to totally take you over is where the issue tends to become a problem.

When you're thinking about your energy before a call or conversation, even a video presentation, it's also worth thinking about what you're thinking before it. If you're repeating to yourself that you can't sell then you need to remind yourself that you absolutely can. If you're repeating to yourself that you're not good enough then you need to remind yourself that you actually are. How you prepare before the call or sales activity has a direct impact on how easy it'll feel and whether you get the YES or a NO.

Of course when we're thinking of the environment it's not just about your energy it's also about the physical environment you are operating in, the physical space in which we are in can also impact our energy, it can also impact the way in which we might be showing up for the activity we're about to do.

Understanding the physical environments in which you operate best is also important. Just because you have an office, for example, doesn't mean that's the best place for you to do sales calls (if you do them). Maybe the environment isn't one that fuels you with the right energy to do that. I know that my office isn't as bright as I'd like all the time. If I am doing a sales call I prefer to head outside in the sunshine. It's where I find myself being fuelled.

I know people who thrive in coffee shop environments

but for me it's the worst possible thing. Of course, if you're in a position where you can't choose the physical environment where you're working from, then you have to work with what you have.

That could mean making changes to the space you use, finding another part of the house or office to do different activities from, or even exploring something such as Creative Feng Shui ®, which is the creation of Sarah Stone.

Sarah has recently totally transformed my work environment and every area of my home. She has also activated all the areas of my home to ensure that not only am I operating from the best physical space but that my home and work spaces are activated in order for me to achieve everything I desire.

In the past I've also re-painted a wall in a room to change the energy that helped the physical space fuel me more and create a better environment for me.

There are plenty of ways in which you can make changes to your environment, whether they're small changes or bigger ones. You could simply have different spaces where you do your sales activity and your creative activity. You could go outside, perhaps. Find what's going to work for you and what's going to help you open up that space you need!

"If you hang out with chickens, you're going to cluck and if you hang out with eagles, you're going to fly."

— *STEVE MARABOLI*

I'm not one of those people who believe that you need to stop speaking to everyone in your family or any friends that aren't as ambitious or don't have the same mindset as you. If I was to do that I'd not speak to anyone other than my entrepreneur friends and my husband.

But it is, of course, about not taking their beliefs, thoughts and energies on as your own. Whilst maintaining relationships with them should you wish, you should also ensure you're expanding your connections in other areas.

We've talked a few times about proof. What better way is there to feel as if you can do something than to surround yourself with people who prove to you that it's possible, people that when you share a goal or when you are struggling with something, aren't going to tear you down or cause further doubt in yourself.

Even if you're someone who has a very open minded family or very positive and supportive friends, surrounding yourself with people who are achieving what you desire or are on the same path as you is one that's highly recommended. I've actually taken courses just so I could surround myself with certain types of people. I didn't really need the course but I did want to be immersed in their world and surrounded by the type of person who was taking part.

This doesn't mean however that you should go and surround yourself with people you don't particularly like. Just because someone might be achieving what you desire or is on the same path as you doesn't mean you're going to vibe with them and doesn't mean you should surround yourself with them.

They still have to be people that you're going to enjoy spending time with; they still have to be people you're going to enjoy surrounding yourself with. Whilst of course it's surrounding yourself with them for your own growth, it won't do your growth much justice if you totally don't vibe with them.

But what does this have to do with selling?

Your circle forms part of your environment - the environment that you're selling from, showing up from, taking action from and it all plays a part in that goal of making sales effortlessly. The more your environment is set up to work in the right way FOR you, the easier you'll actually find everything, and part of your environment is other people.

If the other people in your environment are ones that subtract from it but don't add a whole heap then your environment isn't one that truly fuels you. It's not about having a group of people that stand there every day and cheer you on, but just being surrounded by people with a higher energy can raise yours.

Surrounding yourself with people who are on the same path as you or even achieving what you desire will lift you and your own belief. Surrounding yourself with people who you can talk to and share things with will impact your environment.

When we surround ourselves with people who perhaps don't understand what we're trying to achieve, are negative, have a different mindset, or don't believe in us, we're more likely to not take action, to slip into their energy, to slip into their lack of belief even. But when we surround ourselves with people who are the opposite of all of that, it stands to reason that it has a positive impact on us.

A negative environment will affect your sales in a negative way. A positive environment will affect it in a positive way.

That's not to say that you shouldn't ever speak to anyone else, but when you're surrounded by the right people the words of those others won't actually have the same effect. They won't have a hold over you in the same way and they certainly won't hold you back in the same way that they might if they were the only people you surrounded yourself with.

And as a side note, surrounding yourself with different people can be great for expanding your mind, helping you think outside of the box, challenging you in new ways, even. It helps you grow in so many ways and has the added bonus of helping you sell from a lighter, more positive space resulting in an environment that is great for attracting effortless sales!

Action Points:

What sales goal do you desire to be a done deal?

Who would you be if you were already there?

What would you be doing that you're potentially not currently doing?

What energy fuels you best when selling?

How can you bring that energy into your life?

What do you need to remind yourself of before you go into sales activities?

What's important to have in a physical space that helps create the right environment to fuel you?

What drains you in the current physical spaces where you are selling or showing up from?

What five people would you absolutely love to spend time with and why?

How could you spend more time with those type of people?

Chapter Twelve

DISRUPT

*D*ISRUPT is all you need to remember when thinking about how to sell high-ticket effortlessly. Honestly, it'll make sense in a second, but why DISRUPT? Because disrupting is exactly what has led me to being here today writing this second book: disrupting and blazing my own path, following what's right for me and not what the crowd says I have to do, are exactly why you're here reading this.

So whenever you're feeling heavy about selling, whenever you're feeling the pressure, thinking that selling is hard, comparing yourself to how others sell, wondering how to make sales flow and what the secret to selling really is, just remember DISRUPT!

Destination:

What is your goal? What are you trying to achieve? What's the vision and the destination of where you're looking to get to?

In my first book, She Lives Limitlessly, I talked about the first part of a limitless life. Leveraging high-ticket selling to achieve it is truly understanding your why and what it is you're looking to create.

It's important in every aspect of your high-ticket business, from knowing what it is you want to be selling, to having a model that enables you to earn what you desire whilst living the life you desire, to selling in a way you love. Knowing your vision and your destination is one of the keys to selling high-ticket with ease.

Ideal client:

I know, I know, eye rolls... you've seen this buzz word thrown around the internet until you're blue in the face, right? But you can't sell effortlessly without knowing who your ideal client is and we're talking about knowing them on all levels.

You need to know what they desire so you can sell what they want and stand out. You need to know who it is you're going to work with so you can attract the people you're going to love spending time with and selling to.

You need to know how they love to buy, so you can have a sales process that is perfectly aligned with how they like to buy and what they need to experience in order to buy.

Ideal client is a foundation you simply cannot skip out!

Strategy:

You can have all the wishes and beliefs under the sun, but you are going to need to have a strategy behind all of it that enables you to make sales. It must be a strategy that is built not just for you but for those that are going to be buying from you.

You need a marketing strategy that means you're being seen in the right places, by the right people. You need a lead generation strategy that means you're bringing in those perfect hot leads who cannot wait to buy from you.

Your strategy doesn't have to be complicated, but it does have to focus on you and who it is that you're selling to. Don't create a strategy based on what you see others doing; it works for them but it will only work for you if the strategy is actually going to get you in front of the right people.

Remember, not everyone buys and hangs out on Facebook! There is a big wide world out there and you have to find where your people are and then have the best strategy to get in front of them and have them buy from you

Radiate:

Be the person who shines so bright; be the person who people cannot wait to buy from; be the future you who's already where you desire to be. Be the person who just radiates towards everything you desire.

Believe you can achieve what you desire; know that what you desire is completely safe for you and is available for you if you're ready to claim it.

Step into the mindset that benefits you rather than one that holds you back. Step into the energy that fuels you not one that exhausts you. Step into the environment that helps you radiate and out of one that dulls your sparkle.

What would future you take action on today? Go and do it!

Unapologetic:

Claim your worth and be of full service to your audience / potential clients and unapologetically sell.

Don't shrink yourself out of fear of others not valuing you or seeing your worth. Don't not tell the world you have something to offer in case it offends someone or someone sees you as being salesy. Know that selling is being of service; selling is an extension of the passion you have for what you do. Not letting the world see that means that someone doesn't get to experience or have something that they need.

Ensure that your potential clients know they can buy from you. The door is open for them to walk through. No guessing, no wondering, stand up loud and SELL!

But remember to do it in a way that's right for you. Don't be forced into selling in a way that's out of alignment for you or for your ideal clients because someone else does it another way. Remember, there are a million ways to achieve something and there's a method perfect for everyone.

Selling is just a conversation that can happen in a million different ways!

Positioning:

Position yourself to stand above the noise; position yourself so you stand out from the crowd. What will you specialise in? What will you claim as being yours and elevate your positioning with?

Remember to always position yourself towards the want, desire and destination of your ideal clients and how they see. Sell the want and then give them what they need!

Don't forget to let other people raise your positioning. Let other people tell others and show others that they should connect with you. It's not a mountain you have to climb on your own; others can help you get there.

Transform:

Transform your environment from being one that doesn't fuel you to one that fuels you like a rocket ship towards where you desire to be. Be in tune with the energies that serve you in various circumstances. Know what's going to help you show up with the right energy in order to perform best in every single situation and activity.

Surround yourself with the right people who will help you in your transformation and encourage you to keep growing. Find people who will support you and believe in you even when you have those moments of doubt in yourself. Surround yourself with people who open your eyes to what's possible.

Surround yourself with people who just get it!

Conclusion: Just fucking get out of your way, believe in yourself and disrupt your industry by doing YOU!

DO YOU WANT TO CONTINUE YOUR JOURNEY?

Have I piqued your interest?

Have you taken a peek into my ways, thinking and brain and thought, "I want more!" Then how about we continue the journey?

Sell Five High-Ticket Packages In Under 30 Days FREE Challenge (even with a small audience!)

This free challenge is designed to show you how, even with the smallest of audiences, you can supercharge your sales and sell five high-ticket packages in under thirty days.

Limitless Living Lounge

Come hang out in my private Facebook community where I sometimes do free trainings, challenges and generally drop Jane bombs to brighten up your days, kick your ass and get those AHA moments flowing, to help you unlock your own limitless life and sell high-ticket with ease.

Get access to the above and much more right here on this link:

http://www.iamjanebaker.com/booklinks

She Lives Limitlessly is my first published best-selling book. She Lives Limitlessly shares How To Supercharge Your Results By Selling High End As A Service Based Business Owner or Coach.

Available as an ebook, paperback and hardback. On all Amazon platforms, Waterstones and Barnes & Noble.

I COULDN'T HAVE DONE IT WITHOUT YOU

I still find my journey insane. Sometimes it still doesn't really make much sense to me. Sixteen years ago I was written off as the high school dropout with no plan and no real hope for the future, then pregnant at seventeen, still with no plan, qualifications or job.

Yet here I am, and here you are having finished my second book!

I couldn't finish writing this one without leaving some thank yous.

There's only one person my first thank you could ever go to and that's Abigail Horne from Authors & Co whose support hasn't just meant writing, publishing and becoming a best seller with one book, but here I am writing and publishing my second. I spent years thinking and dreaming about writing a book, but I honestly didn't think I really had anything to share. I wasn't a writer and I didn't even know where to begin.

With Abi and the whole team at Authors & Co I've now been able to realise my dream of writing and publishing a book twice. Without their support and encouragement this wouldn't have happened, so a big thank you to Abi for all of your support, encouragement and dealing with my crazy, ridiculous, last minute ideas. I couldn't ever have done it without you. I'm regularly asked what my proudest achievement is and every time, it's my book. I have you to thank for that. Thank you for helping me achieve one of my proudest moments that I will forever be grateful for!

To all of my clients that I've had the privilege of working with over the years, I don't take anything that I do for granted. I don't take being able to be part of your journey lightly and being trusted to be part of your journey is something I regard as an incredible honour. It brings me so much joy to watch every single one of you grow and achieve your own dreams. When you share your wins I get just as excited by them as I do when I have my own. Without all of you, this journey wouldn't have been possible. Thank you for allowing me to be part of your growth and to witness all of the incredible, amazing things you all do.

Of course, to the readers of this book and my first book,

thank you for buying, for taking time out of your day to read my words, to listen to my thoughts, to learn from my strategies and teachings. I cherish every single one of you.

To my friends, you know who you are! Thank you for being there when I had my crisis moments writing this book and my last one. Thank you for listening when I need to vent and release. Thank you for being my cheerleaders and reminding me that I'm a kick ass superpower when I temporarily forget that I am. Thank you for always reminding me that I can achieve anything. Thank you for just being there... it means more than any of you might ever know!

To my amazing step sister, Chelle... it's funny that there'll be people reading this only just discovering we're step sisters. It actually amuses me every time that happens so that's obviously part of the reason why I'm including you here, but of course it's not the only reason. I still remember when my mother broke the news that she was marrying your father. Let's be honest - I didn't exactly take it very well, but we've come a long way since then. You're the person who's there in a crisis, you listen to my mad ramblings, you're always there no matter what, and you're one of my biggest cheerleaders and partners in crime. Thank you for always having my back and for everything! I love you.

To my mother, I was going to miss you out just because I knew you'd be searching to see if you got a mention! But of course I was going to include you - how could I not? Who'd have thought that you'd be reading a thank you to you in a book that I wrote and published?

No matter what, you have always believed in me. Even when there was no proof I could turn my life around, you never doubted I could. Despite what you may have thought, you never once told me I couldn't do anything, never once told me that I couldn't achieve what I desired, and I consider myself extremely lucky to have a mother like you. Thank you for always believing in me, thank you for trusting me to find my own way even though it didn't look like I knew what I was doing. Thank you for allowing me to be me and find my own way in life. I love you!

To my father, we've not always had the easiest of relationships and our journey definitely hasn't been straightforward, but thank you for encouraging me to always be better. Thank you for the lessons that you probably don't even realise you've helped me learn. Thank you for being part of my journey that has led me here today. Without that I'd probably be living a very different life.

To my amazing children, you may never read this - apparently my books aren't cool enough but, hey, they may be one day, right? Thank you for giving me the greatest role I've ever had and that's being your mother. I know I can be a right pain sometimes and totally uncool because your friends follow me on TikTok, but I love you, all of you, and everything I do is for you, for us. I hope I've showed you that you too can achieve anything. You can always reach your dreams and I will always be there being your biggest cheerleader, no matter what you choose to do in life. Thank you for being my fuel.

And, of course, last but nowhere near least, my husband Lloyd. What a journey we've been on so far. I'm fairly sure you didn't expect our life to turn out like this when we first met. When you first walked into my crazy sixteen year old life I can almost guarantee you didn't think we'd end up here, living an amazing life, that you'd be married to a best-selling author, have a successful business and amazing children, and living on a sunshine island.

But we did it, and I say *we* because this has never just been my journey and I'd never in a million years have achieved half of what I have if it hadn't been for you. You believe in me more than anyone else I know. You've listened to my crazy ideas and then given me the space, encouragement and support to bring them to life. Together we've taken a dream and brought it to life in ways neither of us would have originally imagined possible. Thank you will never ever be enough - you are my absolute best friend, my total soulmate and there is no one I'd want to be on this journey with other than you. Here's to further building our empire, having more amazing memories as a family and unapologetically living our best lives together xx I love you!

ABOUT THE AUTHOR

Jane Baker is a high-ticket sales expert, best-selling author, speaker and entrepreneur. She specialises in helping service based business owners, coaches and persons of influence leverage high-ticket selling to drastically increase their income whilst also unlocking time freedom so they can live limitlessly!

Often described as a disruptor, Jane has spent her life blazing her own path and is now on a path to help others do the same. She's passionate about helping people claim their worth, leverage high-ticket selling to unlock a life they truly desire to live, whilst loving sales and selling in a way that's in total alignment with them.

Jane specialises in working with service based business owners, coaches and also works with high profile persons of influence right across the globe, helping them leverage high-ticket selling in their respective businesses and industries.

Originally from Wales, United Kingdom, Jane now lives in the Canary Islands with her family, although she's a self-confessed travel-holic so is actually usually found somewhere in the sky on her way to their next family adventure somewhere in the world.

You can find out more about Jane and follow her here:

www.iamjanebaker.com

facebook.com/IamJaneBaker
instagram.com/IamJaneBaker
twitter.com/IamJaneBaker